SHAW: THE PLAYS

Desmond MacCarthy

SHAW: THE PLAYS

FOREWORD BY J. W. LAMBERT

DAVID & CHARLES
NEWTON ABBOT

0 7153 6312 3

First published by MacGibbon & Kee in 1951
Reprinted 1951
This edition published by David & Charles in 1973

Printed in Great Britain
by Redwood Press Limited Trowbridge
for David & Charles (Holdings) Limited
South Devon House Newton Abbot Devon

Contents

v

CONTENTS

INSTEAD OF A FOREWORD

INSTEAD OF A FOREWORD

FEW DEVICES in literature are so irritating as the foreword which tells one how to respond to the book which it precedes. I should not be writing this note if I did not greatly admire the criticism of Desmond MacCarthy, but its purpose is to introduce him, however sketchily, to those for whom he is at best a name.

He was born in 1878 of Anglo-Irish, French and German stock. 'In spite,' he said of himself, 'of having been at Eton and Cambridge, I regard myself as a self-educated man'; and indeed for all his seventy-five years, until his death in 1952, he retained the open curiosity—the subject of this book is another prime example of its power—which is the final advantage of the auto-didact over the victim of a fully-fashioned formal education.

Nevertheless, Eton and Cambridge contributed much to the pattern of his life. At Eton he was immersed in the worldliness which, given his temperament, developed an ease of manner and a nose for distinction which enabled him to move easily in almost any society. At Cambridge he was at once accepted by that dazzling élite which included the exuberant, songs-at-the-piano philosopher G. E. Moore, the young Bertrand Russell and Maynard Keynes, E. M. Forster and Lytton Strachey. It was therefore natural that he should become closely associated with the Bloomsbury group whom Mollie, his wife, nicknamed the 'Bloomsberries'.

Yet MacCarthy himself, as a man and as a critic, had little in common with their aesthetically overbred, often dismissive and, at times, malicious attitudes. In innumerable memoirs and letters the same adjectives attach to him again and again—amiable, affable, generous, good-natured. These qualities rather got on Bloomsbury's nerves, as indeed did his effortless capacity to relate art to life, his confidence that criticism should be largely 'discourse upon human nature', rather than mere qualitative assessment in an aesthetic vacuum. Nor has this civility endeared him to Bloomsbury's arch-enemies, our latter-day critical totalitarians, mostly but not entirely to be found in the universities. Apt to refer petulantly to 'the Desmond MacCarthy streak in English letters', they dismiss a style which is at once conversational yet precise, a wit which is always illuminating and never ostentatious ('He was no good at games, not even at rowing—in spite of being a lout'), imagery which always opens our eyes ('A rocking-horse is more like a horse than a photograph of a Derby winner'), and a relentless distaste for pretension, self-satisfied moral indignation (a lifelong liberal himself, he was unfailingly hostile to this most liberal of afflictions) and cruel insensitivity, not least in artists—like Shaw—whom he particularly admired.

I see that I am in some danger of doing what I deplored in my opening sentence. Of MacCarthy on Shaw I will add merely—and as, surely, a matter of demonstrable fact—that his instant responses to Shaw's plays display insight into their lasting essence to a humbling degree; our century twists and turns, but what MacCarthy saw as important in Shaw is what is still seen as important in Shaw, and why we still see Shaw as important.

This is not least remarkable since in no way could MacCarthy be considered a natural Shavian. His unmistakable Irishness was of quite another order—perhaps complementary. He was by temperament elusive, dilatory and conveniently vague. 'I've never seen,' said Lytton Strachey, of all people, 'anyone so extraordinarily incapable of pulling himself together . . . He'll never write anything, I'm afraid, in that hopeless miasma.' And he never did, beyond his critical journalism and a handful of short stories. Perhaps his brilliance as a talker, and the inevitable demands therefore made upon his company, eroded his will to write; perhaps, on the other hand, he deliberately used his conversation and his apparent confusion (not, when closely examined, in the same class as Strachey's psychological chaos) as a barrier behind which he lived exactly the life he wished. The unambitious result, in any case, was a lifetime of acute, humane, uncondescending, shared exploration of art and life alike, in person as in print.

The exasperating old gentleman who, with the final sentences of his weekly article still at the last minute unwritten, was to be found in a corner with two or three *Sunday Times* compositors, gasping with asthma but chuckling over next week's crossword puzzle, was a man to love; and, for my money, a critic to revere.

J. W. Lambert
October 1973

PREFACE BY THE AUTHOR

PREFACE BY THE AUTHOR

I HAVE WRITTEN more about Bernard Shaw than about any other writer living or dead: I was a dramatic critic for over forty years, and if I think how much less interesting my work would have been without Shaw's plays to see and discuss, I am prostrated with gratitude, although gratitude and admiration were not the only emotions I tried to express about each play as it appeared.

The Shaw whom I admired, and whose plays threw so much light on life for me, died a good many years before 1950. After *Saint Joan* (1923), although his plays continued to show here and there his astonishing penetration and originality, none were really good; while on the most fundamental questions he seemed to me wrong, and often in flat contradiction to his earlier self.

What Voltaire was in Europe in 1778, the year of his death, Shaw is in the world today. Like Voltaire, he has been all his long life a perpetual fountain of wit, intellectual energy and controversy. A rationalist without reverence, he too attacked the churches while proclaiming the necessity of religion; he, too, was a mocker of tradition, a fearless defender of the victims of legality and a champion of causes in disgrace; a humanitarian with a poor opinion of men: benevolent without love. Only, unlike Voltaire, Shaw was as free as a saint from pettiness and spite.

In economics Shaw consistently stuck to Socialism as civilisation's one remedy, and to equalitarian Socialism as the foundation of morals—at any rate in his prefaces and essays. Yet his creative imagination was a crow which followed many furrows, and outside economics his philosophy, like Voltaire's, might be described as a chaos of clear ideas. Oddly enough, both men have been remarkable for never having said about anything "I do not know", while both were regarded as the leading dramatists of their age. We speak in retrospect of "The Age of Voltaire". If posterity does not speak of the last forty years as "the Shavian Age" it will not be because Shaw has had less influence, but because the world has become far larger and more complex, so that no one writer can be thought of as dominating it. It is, by the way, impossible for us to think of Shaw's plays becoming so utterly outmoded as Voltaire's. He put far more of his genius into them than Voltaire ever did into his.

Although Shaw the thinker cannot be separated from Shaw the dramatist, they are seldom identical. The themes of his prefaces are often only of minor importance in the plays themselves.

Shaw, the dramatist, began with Fabian attacks on social abuses; landlordism in *Widowers' Houses*, financially organised prostitution in *Mrs. Warren's Profession*. The Ibsen-theme of the marriage market and women's enslavement supplies contributory themes in other plays. For a while the anti-romantic conception of love is his leading theme. Then, suddenly, he chucks all half-measures over and in *Man and Superman* proclaims that there is only one hope; eugenics. Man must be born again and born different. It logically follows, from the assertion that the child is the sole end of marriage, that it is absurd to make it binding, and that the State should breed from good stock.

We never hear again of this fundamental remedy. On the contrary, in *Major Barbara* a different one is proposed. In his earlier *Caesar and Cleopatra* Shaw's faith in the powerful leader, rather than in the people, had peeped out. In *Major Barbara* it became more explicit, and in some of his latest plays, notably in *The Apple Cart*, it became emphatic.

But meanwhile in *Back to Methuselah* another universal remedy was suggested: men will never improve till they learn to live so long that their passions and instincts wither, leaving them all brain. But subsequently we hear no more of *that* solution of all ills.

In his last plays, from *The Apple Cart* onwards, the problem which lies before civilisation is seen as the need to discover how the community can distribute more fairly the wealth it produces, and how it can best choose its rulers.

This incomplete outline of Bernard Shaw's development as a philosophic dramatist sketches a pattern worth keeping in mind. His peculiar gifts as a playwright are too numerous for mention here. But three must be recalled. His extraordinary gift for presenting different types; his ability to lend each in turn, when the points of view clash, his own brilliant powers of expression; and of course, his glorious intellectual high spirits —that fountain of lovely gaiety which went on playing however gloomy the state of the world.

November, 1950

The dates at the head of the essays indicate when they were first published. Grateful acknowledgement is made by author and publishers to Messrs. Sidgwick & Jackson, Ltd., for the right to reprint the early essays from Mr. MacCarthy's *The Court Theatre*, published by A. H. Bullen (1907); to the editor of *The New Statesman and Nation* for permission to reprint other early essays from *The Speaker* and all the later essays which appeared in *The New Statesman and Nation* itself; to the staff of the same paper for much kind assistance in collecting the essays; and lastly to *The Sunday Times* for permission to use a recent appreciation of Shaw. Permission to use extracts from the plays has been granted by the Public Trustee and the Society of Authors.

AT THE COURT THEATRE

MR SHAW'S CHARACTERS

1907

MR BERNARD SHAW is a difficult subject for criticism: there is so much to discuss, and yet so much has been already said; there are so many interesting things to say about his work which are not quite true, and so many true things which are not interesting; and to crown all, he has explained himself many times. Before dealing with the plays themselves I propose in this chapter to discuss first their characters and secondly, the treatment of the emotions in them.

There is one characteristic of Mr Shaw's imaginative work which, oddly enough, has not been commented upon; perhaps it has been considered too obvious for comment. It is the exceptional variety and vividness of his characters. They have too, a peculiar quality, which makes them stay in the memory, and enables them to pass, like the types of Dickens, into conversation. For instance, 'Enery Straker, Prossy, Broadbent, 'B. B.', Ann (to rob her of that philosophic universality which her creator claims for her), all possess this quality. Once seen on the stage, they become types in the spectator's imagination, approximations to which he is constantly meeting in real life. Any one, for instance, would be understood directly who said, 'I travelled up in the train to-day with a little mechanic—a sort of 'Enery Straker.' Such characters are drawn by constantly bringing into relief one distinguishing feature, too complex perhaps to be defined, in such a way that the imagination instinctively supplies all the other qualities. It is the triumph of the playwright to achieve this intense simplification, and if the Shavian theatre is compared with the work of other modern playwrights in this respect, its superiority is overwhelmingly apparent.

In psychological observation, Mr Shaw has a caricaturist's

3

quickness in seizing the salient feature; but this is combined in him with a constant sense that the stuff of human nature is much the same in every one. The kind of distinctness which his characters possess differs, consequently, from the distinctness which the old school of psychological dramatists achieved. They were always seeking for 'the ruling passion' in their men and women, and making them act accordingly, thus in effect dividing mankind into species—the proud man, the miser, the libertine, etc. Mr Shaw emphasises, on the other hand, that men are at bottom swayed by the same common impulses, and that their behaviour is generally what circumstances, education, and the treatment they receive from others at the moment make it; he never fails, therefore, to suggest that society is responsible for their misdeeds as well as for their oddities. As a social reformer, he has theorised upon and analysed the effect of this or that social environment on life and character; as an artist he has always been preoccupied with human nature. These two preoccupations, working together, have enabled him to seize with extraordinary quickness the traces which a particular manner of living leave on a personality. His figures are often exaggerated; but in nine instances out of ten they are saved from being pointlessly fantastic by the fact that they are closely linked with social conditions. As a propagandist, again, he has perpetually been in violent collision with many people holding different points of view; and as an observer he has noted the particular mental, physical, and social characteristics which usually go with particular ways of looking at the world. Such experience is of the utmost value to the dramatist; for drama depends upon the clash between characters who embody different points of view. If on both sides the difference is one of conflicting desires, that is one kind of drama; but it becomes often more interesting when the opposing wills represent whole groups of ideas by which many men hold and live. Such is the interest of the contest between the poet and the parson, over which Candida stands as umpire; of the discussions between Larry and Broadbent, and of the blind *melée* at the end of *John Bull's Other Island* between them and Father Keegan; of the explosive interview between Roebuck and Tanner: of the sharp passage-of-arms between Undershaft and 'the honest poor man' Peter Shirley, and of many other spirited encounters. In all these scenes, what impresses us is the hammer-and-tongs vigour with which each combatant stands up for his side, and the natural congruity of his outlook with the sort of person his general behaviour shows him to be.

Mr Shaw is a most striking refutation of the notion that an artist gets the best work out of himself when he holds aloof from the social and religious questions of his day; the artist in him owes an enormous debt to the reformer.

Those characters which strike us as exceptional rather than typical have the same distinctions. Among them Tanner, Valentine, Charteris, and Undershaft are particularly interesting to the analyst, because they combine in varying degrees the temperament and opinions which tell most in Mr Shaw's writings when he speaks for himself. Tanner and Undershaft have definite systematic views upon morals and politics and human nature; and though Valentine and Charteris have not, they are all four 'realists', that is to say, they are not under what Mr Shaw considers 'romantic illusions'. Valentine and Charteris would be easy converts to the complete doctrine. Valentine shares the fate of Tanner in being swallowed up in matrimony, and although he betrays a flutter of trepidation before the persistence of the young woman whose feelings he has just taken by storm, he evidently has never had the true inward horror of his frightful predicament clearly revealed to him. Poor Charteris has even some misgivings about his escape from a similar quandary. It is true there is a touch of irony in his lament upon losing Grace Tranfield, which betrays a glimmering of philosophy, but there is also more than a trace of regret: Grace Tranfield was not such a one as Ann Whitefield.

5

'Yes; this is the doom of the philanderer. I shall have to go on philandering now all my life. No domesticity, no fireside, no little ones—nothing at all in Cuthbertson's line.' The irony here has two edges.

But there is a second quality common to all these leading characters, unmistakable but harder to describe. It is a temperamental quality, which, by the way, makes these parts extremely hard to act: they are always on the verge of a state of lyrical excitement. Sometimes it takes the form of a sudden towering of high spirits, sometimes of a good-natured combative ecstasy, sometimes of explosive indignation. It differs in each character, but in all it is the same kind of emotion—a sudden sense of freedom and certainty, bringing with it sudden fluency and emphasis of speech, and a feeling of immunity and detachment, which is at the same time a state of extreme emotional mobility. Undershaft takes such moments very solemnly, he is certain he is 'saved'; to Valentine they are whiffs of blind exhilarating joy; to the poet in *Candida* (who has the temperamental quality but does not share such opinions) they are inspirations; to Cusins (who also does not hold them) they are the moments when as a philosophic juggler he can keep all his bowls and basins spinning their fastest, when he can remember the point of twenty creeds at once, and of his love for Barbara into the bargain. To Tanner they are opportunities for psychological declamation.

All authors of merit give to their creations an excess of some characteristic which is dominant in themselves. Thus Mr Meredith's characters are filled to an unnatural degree with the beauty and courage of life; Balzac gives to his a treble dose of will and appetite; the men and women in Mr James's novels, the stupid as well as the intelligent, show a far subtler power of perception than such men and women would actually have. In the same way, Mr Shaw gives to many of his principal characters temperaments which are marked by both extreme mobility and extreme detachment.

6

Sometimes this gift of himself on the part of a writer is more obviously diffused over the whole of his work than concentrated in characters. *The Tempest*, and, to add a modern example, some of the novels of Mr Thomas Hardy, are instances. This is what we mean by creating 'an atmosphere,' when we use that word in a sense of high æsthetic praise, and not simply in order to indicate that the author has succeeded in giving us the sensation of particular scenes or surroundings. Here Mr Shaw's work (though he is extremely skilful in creating 'atmosphere' in the other sense) is deficient, and consequently it is not sufficiently admired by people who are quick to see its other merits, but delight above all things in this quality.

His plays, with the exception, perhaps, of *You Never Can Tell*, are the outcome of his imagination working along the lines which his opinions have already laid down, rather than free expressions of his artistic temperament; with the result that those plays are the best to the making of which has gone the most hard, consistent thinking; and those in which the underlying thought is indistinct are, as wholes, most inferior to passages and characters in them—and, indeed, sometimes inferior to the work of inferior writers.

With regard to the characters which are neither 'types' nor combinations, in varying proportions, of his own views and temperament, there are two obvious points to notice. Firstly, that all the women are astonishingly real—and how few dramatists can draw more than two or three women well! Candida, Nora Reilly, Lady Cecily Waynflete, Mrs Clandon, Lady Britomart, are as different as possible; yet we know how they would behave under any circumstances. Secondly, the completeness with which such characters as Larry Doyle (a very subtle study), William the waiter, the Rev. James Morell are presented, and the distinctness of such minor figures as Crampton, Mrs Whitefield, Father Dempsey, Roebuck Ramsden, Barney Doran, Mr Malone the elder, and Octavius Robinson.

If the reader will review in imagination all the personages mentioned in this section, he will find it hard to parallel in any other dramatist a list so various, so new to the stage, so easy to recognize and to remember.

Next to the force with which original characters are presented, the most noticeable feature in Mr Shaw's work is his treatment of emotion, and especially of sexual emotion. What first strikes us in the Shavian theatre is, perhaps, the frequency of excited scenes, of explosive arguments, violent protestations, gesticulations and agitations. Apart from the recurrence of abstract discussions and the vigour of the dialogue there would be nothing very strange in this excitement, were not the passions and emotions, so violently displayed, represented as being also startlingly brief. This emphasis upon brevity of emotion is very characteristic, and one cause of the charge of cynicism which is so often brought against him. The typical scene is one in which the characters are represented in violent states of moral indignation, rage, perplexity, mortification, infatuation, despair, which subside as suddenly as they rose. The Shavian hero is a man who does not take all this hubble-bubble for more than it is worth. He preserves an exasperating good humour through it, however energetic his retorts may be, because he reckons on human nature being moved, in the long run, only by a few fundamental considerations and instincts. The hostility which he excites does not therefore trouble him in the least. He counts upon the phenomenon, ultimately working in his favour, that puzzles Tanner in himself when confronted with Ann; that is, upon the contradiction between moral judgments and instinctive likings and respect. Valentine is not dismayed by Gloria's disapproval, nor Bluntschli by Raina's contempt for his lack of conventionally soldier-like qualities; both are confident that the ultimate decisions of these ladies will depend on other things. Even Tanner soon finds himself on excellent terms with Roebuck Ramsden, who began by abusing him as an infamous fellow. But it is not merely the fact that the confidence of the 'realists' is always justified in the plays which emphasises the instability of human emotions and judgments; this is one of the fundamental assumptions with regard to human nature which lie at the back of the plays themselves. It is one of the chief reasons, too, why they are regarded as fantastic; for the normal instability of emotion has hitherto found very little reflection in literature or on the stage; vacillations, flaggings, changes of mind and inconsequences of thought having been generally confined to characters intended to be obviously weak. But Mr Shaw represents, quite truly, characters of considerable firmness in many respects as subject to them.

In common with all writers of comedy he depends for his effects upon the contradictions between what people say they believe and how they act; but for his surprises and fun he draws more than most writers on the normal instability of feeling.

A great deal of comedy rests upon the weakness of emotions and aspirations in conflict with instincts and necessities; a hungry lover, for instance, thinking more of his breakfast than his mistress, is a comic figure; so is an indignant husband being petted into acquiescence. But whether or not we laugh happily at such scenes, depends upon the spirit in which they are treated. If this spirit is one of censure and contempt for the weakness of emotion, the scene becomes satire at once; but if the scene is presented in such a way that we recognize the infirmity of human nature, which nevertheless still seems lovable, it remains comedy; and comedy may include anything from the most boisterous fun to the tenderest irony.

Mr Shaw's plays are a curious mixture of comedy and satire. The spirit that prevails is usually one of remorseless scrutiny into the sincerity and consistency of emotions and motives, and therefore one of satire; but the severity of the decision in each individual case is considerably mitigated by the fact that practically every one else is also found guilty, so that the general impression is that of comedy. He puzzles people by appearing at the same time very hard on human nature, and very indulgent to it. His own explanation of the matter is that his ethics are different from the current morality. He says, in effect, 'If I were to judge you all by the standards your own conscience sets up, which by the bye you are always revoking with extraordinary inconsistency, I should have to condemn you all as more or less worthless; however, I do not judge you according to those principles, but by others of my own.' What these standards are will become clearer when we are examining the plays one by one.

Meanwhile, if 'ira' is represented in these plays as a 'brevis furor', what is 'amor'? In his preface to *Man and Superman*, Mr Shaw says that 'though we have plenty of dramas with heroes and heroines who are in love and must accordingly marry or perish at the end of the play, or about people whose relations with one another have been complicated by the marriage laws, not to mention the looser sort of plays which trade on the tradition that illicit love affairs are at once vicious and delightful, we have no modern English plays in which the natural attraction of the sexes for one another is made the mainspring of the action. . . . What is the usual formula for such plays? A woman has on some past occasion been brought into conflict with the law that regulates the relations of the sexes. A man by falling in love with her, or marrying her, is brought into conflict with the social convention which discountenances the woman. Now the conflicts of individuals with law and convention can be dramatised like all other human conflicts; but they are purely judicial.' The reason why such plays are usually so depressing and uninteresting, he argues, is that they are at bottom utterly sexless. We are really more interested in the relations between the man and the woman, which are slurred over, than in the relations between both and the law.

Elsewhere,[1] however, he has complained that the attraction

[1] The Preface to *Plays for Puritans*.

of the sexes for one another has been made far too much of as 'the mainspring of the action;' everything the hero ever does being represented as done for the sake of the woman he loves. His quarrel with modern English dramatists is then, first, that they represent a passion as pervasively effective in practical affairs which is all-powerful only in day-dreams; and secondly, that they do not represent the nature of this passion directly and frankly. His own plays are not open to either objection. In *Man and Superman* he set out purposely to write a play in which sexual attraction should be the main interest; but in his other plays also he has always made the nature of the attraction between his characters quite clear. What is remarkable about the scenes in which this is done is the extent to which sexual passion is isolated from all other sentiments and emotions. His lovers, instead of using the language of admiration and affection, in which this passion is so often cloaked, simply convey by their words the kind of mental tumult they are in. Sexual attraction is stript bare of all the accessories of poetry and sympathy. It is represented as it is by itself, with its own peculiar romance, but with none of the feelings which may, and often do, accompany it. Take for example the scene between Valentine and Gloria in *You Never Can Tell*.

GLORIA [*uneasily, rising*]. Let us go back to the beach.
VALENTINE [*darkly—looking up at her*]. What! you feel it too?
GLORIA. Feel what?
VALENTINE. Dread.
GLORIA. Dread!
VALENTINE. As if something were going to happen. It came over me suddenly just before you proposed that we should run away to the others.
GLORIA [*amazed*]. That's strange—very strange! I had the same presentiment.
VALENTINE. How extraordinary! [*Rising*]. Well: shall we run away?
GLORIA. Run away! Oh no: that would be childish. [*She sits down again. He resumes his seat beside her, and watches her with*

a gravely sympathetic air. She is thoughtful and a little troubled as she adds] I wonder what is the scientific explanation of those fancies that cross us occasionally!

VALENTINE. Ah, I wonder! It's a curiously helpless sensation: isn't it?

GLORIA [*rebelling against the word*]. Helpless?

VALENTINE. Yes. As if Nature, after allowing us to belong to ourselves and do what we judged right and reasonable for all these years, were suddenly lifting her great hand to take us—her two little children—by the scruffs of our little necks, and use us, in spite of ourselves, for her own purposes, in her own way.

VALENTINE. . . . Oh, I know you mustn't tell me whether you like me or not: but——

GLORIA [*her principles up in arms at once*]. *Must* not? Why not? I am a free woman: why should I not tell you?

VALENTINE [*pleading in terror and retreating*]. Don't. I'm afraid to hear.

GLORIA [*no longer scornful*]. You need not be afraid. I think you are sentimental and a little foolish; but I like you.

VALENTINE [*dropping into the iron chair as if crushed*]. Then it's all over. [*He becomes the picture of despair.*]

GLORIA [*puzzled, approaching him*]. But why?

VALENTINE. Because liking is not enough. Now that I think down into it seriously, I don't know whether I like you or not.

GLORIA [*looking down at him with wondering concern*]. I'm sorry.

VALENTINE [*in an agony of restrained passion*]. Oh, don't pity me. Your voice is tearing my heart to pieces. Let me alone, Gloria. You go down into the very depths of me, troubling and stirring me—I can't struggle with it—I can't tell you——

GLORIA [*breaking down suddenly*]. Oh, stop telling me what you feel: I can't bear it.

VALENTINE [*springing up triumphantly, the agonised voice now solid, ringing and jubilant*]. Ah, it's come at last—my moment of courage. [*He seizes her hands: she looks at him in terror.*] *Our* moment of courage! [*He draws her to him, and kisses her with impetuous strength, and laughs boyishly.*] Now you've done it, Gloria. It's all over: we're in love with one another. [*She can only gasp at him.*] But what a dragon you were! And how hideously afraid I was!

12

Turn now to the final scene between Ann and Tanner:

> TANNER. The will is yours then! The trap was laid from the beginning.
>
> ANN [*concentrating all her magic*]. From the beginning—from our childhood—for both of us—by the Life Force.
>
> TANNER. I will not marry you. I will not marry you.
>
> ANN. Oh, you will, you will.
>
> TANNER. I tell you, no, no, no.
>
> ANN. I tell you, yes, yes, yes.
>
> TANNER. No.
>
> ANN [*coaxing—imploring—almost exhausted*]. Yes. Before it is too late for repentance. Yes.
>
> TANNER [*struck by the echo from the past*]. When did all this happen to me before? Are we two dreaming?
>
> ANN [*suddenly losing her courage, with an anguish that she does not conceal*]. No. We are awake; and you have said no: that is all.
>
> TANNER [*brutally*]. Well?
>
> ANN. Well, I made a mistake: you do not love me.
>
> TANNER [*seizing her in his arms*]. It is false: I love you. The Life Force enchants me: I have the whole world in my arms when I clasp you. But I am fighting for my freedom, my honour, for myself, one and indivisible.

In both these scenes sexual attraction is isolated and separated from feelings of affection and admiration. The only difference between them is that Tanner struggles to hold himself back and Valentine goes in headlong. The amorous experiences of the Philanderer, of Blanche and Trench [*Widowers' Houses*], of Frank and Vivie [*Mrs Warren's Profession*] are treated in exactly the same manner; only in these cases the lover does not analyse or understand his own emotion. This emotion must be distinguished from lust on the one hand, and from love on the other; for in the first place, it is imaginative as well as sensual, an excitement of the mind as well as of the body—of the whole living being in fact—and, in the second, it does not include a desire for the other person's welfare, nor the conscious contemplation of what is good. Valentine and Tanner know that it is a brief or very intermittent emotion, that it has nothing to do with a perception of the beauty of mind or character; hardly, in Tanner's case, with a perception of bodily beauty: Ann's looks were not the kind of beauty which signified much to him. Like his prototype Don Juan when in love, his ear and eye probably tore her voice and looks to pieces; like him he could say, 'My judgment was not corrupted: my brain still said no on every issue. And whilst I was in the act of framing my excuses to the lady, Life seized me and threw me into her arms as a sailor throws a scrap of fish into the mouth of a sea-bird.'[1]

The merit of all these scenes is that they convey with perfect clearness the emotion which possesses the characters, so that it is recognized at once as a real one, and one which has been sentimentally identified with other emotions to the devastation of literature and the confusion of life. The artistic merit of such work requires no comment, and its social importance lies in helping people to distinguish better between their emotions and therefore to walk more surefootedly through life. But at this point Mr Shaw's peculiar bias comes in. His principal intellectual failing, so it seems to me, is to exaggerate the stupidity of mankind. No other writers, not even Carlyle or Tolstoi, appears so convinced that the mistakes and confusions of thought, of which men are guilty, are an absurd, glaring, staring set of elementary blunders. So with regard to the emotion of love, he says in so many words—"You have idealised and sentimentalised love. I will show you what that emotion is. Come, rub your eyes; look at it; isn't that what you mean by "being in love"? Have you the folly to say now that it is worth more than anything else in the world?' And we look, and admit we have often called precisely that emotion 'being in love', and that it was never better represented; but we feel, especially now we see it so clearly, it was not *that* emotion after all to which we gave such importance, but that there is still something very difficult to define to which this value justly

---

[1] *Don Juan in Hell* (*Act III of Man and Superman* as published).

belongs. Nor do we mean then by love the impartial sympathy and kindness which Lady Cecily Waynflete feels towards every one she meets; that is a rare and beautiful quality, and very romantic when it is so constant as it is in her, but that is not it. What Cusins is indicated as feeling in *Major Barbara* is much more like it; but notice now where Mr Shaw's bias comes in. He sums up Cusins's feelings for Barbara by saying, 'By the operation of some instinct which is not merciful enough to blind him with the illusions of love, he is obstinately bent on marrying her.' As an artist, he has put into their behaviour together a great deal more than this; but as a writer of analytical stage-directions and philosophic prefaces, he will not admit that it is more than a case of Tanner and Ann or Valentine and Gloria over again. It is perfectly clear that Cusins, while as a critical observer he may be quite aware of Barbara's faults, and while he is attracted to her instinctively, also feels that happiness in the contemplation of her mind and character and the expression of them in her person, which is included in the common conception of love. But Mr Shaw's contempt for the shoddy confusions of passionate literature, his knowledge of the ease with which men deceive themselves at these junctures, and his constant prejudice that the ordinary view must be hopelessly beside the point, lead him as a philosophical critic to ignore emotional complications, which as an artist he here reflects in his work; and these complications, carried vaguely in the ordinary man's mind, prevent him from being satisfied by Mr Shaw's demonstration that love between the sexes has little or no value in itself, and no significance except as a trustworthy indication by the Life Force that the offspring of that particular union are likely to be sound.

I have discussed the treatment of the emotions as exhibited in these plays at some length, and especially those of love and sexual attraction; because one general impression which Mr Shaw's work leaves behind is that of a loveless world in which actions, which seem the result of affection, are explained as having other causes. On nearer inspection this impression appears to be due to the natural trend of his powers rather than to limitations of feeling. His mission is not to glorify what is best in human nature, but to make men scrutinise their pretensions, their emotions, and their conscience. He satirises rather their virtues and the emotions of which they are proud than the faults to which they would cry 'peccavi'. But he is apt to weaken his case by ignoring the sound element in the emotions and qualities he attacks, and sometimes we find him honouring in one place the very quality he attacked elsewhere as a vice masquerading as a virtue. For instance, he attacks (in *Major Barbara*) the emotion of sympathy for suffering and helplessness which he honours in *Captain Brassbound's Conversion*. Perhaps he would say that Barbara and Lady Cecily did not feel pity; but without compassion, their kindness would have been more patronising and less effectual than the sentimental pity he detests as insufferably morbid and condescending. Again, he jeers at unselfishness, exhorting every man to fight for his own hand irrespective of consequences to others in the one play; and in the other he explains the secret of power as a forgetfulness of self. True, the unselfishness he attacks is part humbug and part feebleness, the kind which make a person a nuisance by compelling all who have to do with him to look after his interests as well as their own; and what Mr Shaw means is simply that you must help yourself, if you are to help others. But he does not give his fellow-men the credit for seeing these distinctions, and he thinks apparently that they will only take the lesson if he ignores them himself for the sake of emphasis. He asserts that forgiveness is a disastrous principle, and in the same book advocates that every man, whatever he may have done, should have the chance of being treated as though he were still capable of decent conduct and feelings, which is the essence of forgiveness. He pours contempt on humility as a kind of perverted emotional luxury or shirking, and yet one of the qualities for which he shows most sympathy is the sense of

16

proportion that makes a man consider his own emotional struggles and catastrophes, or even his own moral progress and refinement, as after all of small consequence compared to the total effect of his conduct in a world bursting with misery. What is this if it is not humility? These contradictions do not spring from a confused view of life; but from the persuasion that he is writing for a world of fools, who are so dense and inert, that they can only be startled into attention; who, being incapable of keeping separate things distinct, are also incapable of being moved by anything but emphatic one-sided statement. It is this conviction which mars much of his work; for it is not true. The ordinary man feels many more distinctions than he can express. Though he may be unable always to refute Mr Shaw he does feel that a great many important things have been left out in dealing with human nature and society, and therefore he is inclined to ignore him as a maker of paradoxes, or merely to enjoy him as a wit. If Mr Shaw had felt more constantly the truth of his own maxim: 'The difference between the shallowest routiner and the deepest thinker appears, to the latter, trifling; to the former, infinite'—for presumably the thinker sees the truth in this matter also better than the ordinary man—his work would have been more convincing. Nevertheless, the influence of clearness and emphatic presentation, and of a point of view extremely well stated, must always be wide. It is a great thing to have a side of things so vividly expressed that you can turn to the author at any time in confidence that you will find in him its most absolute and forcible expression. It is one of the chief causes of lasting reputation. As to Mr Shaw's influence upon his contemporaries, this is best measured by noting how frequently in reading or talking you come across a view of things, which makes you think, 'I wonder whether that is derived from Bernard Shaw;' or by a still subtler test, by watching how often in your private ruminations upon some experience or other the suggestion crosses your mind, 'Was my view of my own feelings coloured by such and such a scene in Shaw's plays or novels?' You may say 'Yes—and a reason for distrusting it;' but whether you say that, or whether you marvel at his insight, the fact that the idea occurs at all is a sign that he is an author of real significance.

CANDIDA

MISS JANET ACHURCH and Mr Charrington had taken *Candida* round the provinces some years before it was produced at the Court Theatre in 1904. The most striking feature in the Court performance was Mr Granville Barker's acting of the poet, Eugene Marchbanks; excepting this, and the acting of Miss Sydney Fairbrother, who represented perfectly the pert, self-respecting honesty and suppressed sentimental devotion of the little cockney typist, it was not better than the earlier rendering.

Candida is the story of the love of a poet, age eighteen, for a practical, clear-headed, sympathetic woman, who has been married some years to a hard-working, socialistic clergyman, with a tremendous gift for moral exhortation. He is a perfectly sincere man, in the sense that he has never uttered a word which he did not honestly believe to be sincere at the time. But in order to get the maximum energy out of himself he has avoided probing himself or examining his relations towards others. His habitual behaviour and utterances would come therefore under the head of what Carlyle called 'sincere cant'. He is certainly a good man, and believes himself to be a strong one. He is devoted to his wife, who returns his affection; but he regards himself as her protector, and the adoration with which his fellow-workers look up to him, and the influence he wields from platform and pulpit have blinded him to the fact that he is really the weaker of the two. She, on the other hand, is well aware of this, and it increases her love for him to feel he needs her help.

Into this household comes the poet, who is so sensitive to the attitudes of the people towards him and the emotional atmosphere of the moment, that he is almost helpless in practical matters. He is a shrinking, embarrassed creature, who appeals to Candida's tenderness at first as an adorer, whom she can shelter and protect. But she soon becomes aware of a side of him which goes near to alarming her once or twice, just as it disturbs poor 'Prossy', and ends by terrifying Morell. In fact, it would frighten her too, were she not at bottom the most matter-of-fact of the four. Candida has a good deal of George Sand in her. She has a great admiration for intense emotion and poetic sensibility; but you feel that the only things she really believes in are the obvious things, which plain people value most, a happy fireside, hard regular work and practical kindness. There is, really, no plumbing the depths of her condescension towards the ideals of a poet. Marchbanks appeals to her as Chopin and Musset appealed to George Sand; while thinking that she sympathises with him completely, she really only sympathises in so far as she can mother and comfort him. Nevertheless, she is immensely grateful to him for understanding her situation, and enjoys his adoration without being moved by it. She realises at the end that he must stand alone; for, like a genuine poet, he is incorruptibly sincere and will not be satisfied with less than ambrosial food. Living in a world of emotions, and understanding them, he is strong where others are weak. The Rev. James Morell begins by laughing patronisingly at what he considers a case of calf-love—and, too, he feels so sure of Candida. The dialogue between them is one of the truest and most spirited Mr Shaw has written. It is magnificent.

Morell rapidly begins to realise that this love is something more serious than he expected; and still sonorously self-complacent, though keeping up with more and more difficulty an attitude of brotherly forbearance, he proceeds to crush the poet with lofty reproaches and moral harangues, which, alas, have a fatal platform ring about them. They are powerful enough in their way (Mr Shaw does not secure the poet's victory by undermining his adversary beforehand), but they are nothing to the terrible directness of Marchbank's retorts, every one making a breach in the parson's self-confidence which hitherto he thought justly based and impregnable. But his habit of attacking others from the pulpit has unfitted him for a close-quarters grapple with an adversary whose sincerity is profounder than his own. He begins to feel his own weakness, and the fear seizes him that perhaps the poet is right, and that while he was rousing meetings to enthusiasm by his emotional oratory his wife may have despised him in her heart. He loses self-control and shakes Marchbanks by the collar, who screams in nervous terror.

MARCHBANKS. . . . [*Morell grasps him powerfully by the lapel of his coat: he cowers down on the sofa and screams passionately.*] Stop, Morell: if you strike me I'll kill myself: I won't bear it. [*Almost in hysterics.*] Let me go. Take your hand away.

MORELL [*with slow emphatic scorn*]. You little snivelling cowardly whelp. [*He releases him.*] Go, before you frighten yourself into a fit.

MARCHBANKS [*on the sofa, gasping, but relieved by the withdrawal of Morell's hand*]. I'm not afraid of you: it's you who are afraid of me.

MORELL [*quietly, as he stands over him*]. It looks like it, doesn't it?

MARCHBANKS [*with petulant vehemence*]. Yes, it does. [*Morell turns away contemptuously. Eugene scrambles to his feet and follows him.*] You think because I shrink from being brutally handled—because [*with tears in his voice*] I can do nothing but cry with rage when I am met with violence—because I can't lift a heavy trunk down from the top of a cab like you—because I can't fight you for your wife as a navvy would: all that makes you think I am afraid of you. But you're wrong. If I haven't got what you call British pluck, I haven't British cowardice either: I'm not afraid of a clergyman's ideas. I'll fight your ideas. I'll rescue her from her slavery to them: I'll pit my own ideas against them. You are driving me out of the house because you daren't let her choose between your ideas and mine. You are afraid to let me see her again. [*Morell, angered, turns suddenly on him. He flies to the door in involuntary dread.*] Let me alone, I say. I'm going.

MORELL [*with cold scorn*]. Wait a moment. I'm not going to touch you: don't be afraid. When my wife comes back she will want to know why you have gone. And when she finds that you are never going to cross our threshold again, she will want to have that explained too. Now I don't wish to distress her by telling her that you have behaved like a blackguard.

MARCHBANKS [*coming back with renewed vehemence*]. You shall—you must. If you give any explanation but the true one, you are a liar and a coward. Tell her what I said; and how you were strong and manly, and shook me as a terrier shakes a rat; and, how I shrank and was terrified; and how you called me a snivelling little whelp and put me out of the house. If you don't tell, I will: I'll write it to her.

MORELL [*taken aback*]. Why do you want her to know this?

MARCHBANKS [*with lyric rapture*]. Because she will understand me, and know that I understand her. If you keep back one word of it from her—if you are not ready to lay the truth at her feet as I am—then you will know to the end of your days that she really belongs to me and not to you. Good-bye.

MORELL [*terribly disquieted*]. Stop: I will not tell her.

MARCHBANKS [*turning near the door*]. Either the truth or a lie you *must* tell her if I go.

MORELL [*temporising*]. Marchbanks: it is sometimes justifiable——

MARCHBANKS [*cutting him short*]. I know—to lie. It will be useless. Good-bye, Mr. Clergyman. [*As he turns finally to the door, it opens, and Candida enters in her housekeeping dress.*]

There are no explanations for the present. In the last act Morell and the poet confront her together, and demand that she shall choose between them. Candida with ironical acquiescence consents, and proposes that they should make their bids for her. Her husband in the vein of proud, manly humility offers her his strength for her protection, his honesty of purpose for her surety, his industry for her living, etc.

CANDIDA [*quite quietly*]. And you, Eugene? What do you offer?

MARCHBANKS. My weakness! my desolation! my heart's need!

CANDIDA. That's a good bid, Eugene. Now I know how to make
   my choice——

and she chooses 'the weaker'. Morell collapses, thinking it is
all over, but the poet knows in a moment that the sentence has
gone against him.

The play ends with an explanation from Candida why
Morell is weak and Eugene strong. The poet goes away without
bitterness, and husband and wife fall into each other's arms.
But, we are told, that neither of them know the secret which is
in the poet's heart. This secret, however, is easy to divine; it
is the knowledge that the love which those two have for each
other is not what he wants or envies, or, to put it prosaically,
it is a contempt for roseate domesticity.

The play is among the best Mr Shaw has written. The
interest is concentrated on the main theme throughout, and
it finishes at the point from which the audience, looking back,
can best understand all that has happened, which cannot be
said of his last two plays. It is the first play to show what is
becoming more and more obvious in his writings, that, in
addition to the rationalistic point of view from which he
criticises conventions and social institutions, he looks on the
world from another, which is defiantly and ruthlessly idealistic.
As a socialist, he is always attempting to prove that social and
moral conventions must be broken up and changed because
they do not lead to human happiness; but his favourable judgment of individuals depends upon the extent to which they
despise and dispense with happiness themselves. In personal
relations, in love, he apparently sees little value; love is a
comfort, a consoling kind of happiness, which a great man can
do without; when he is tired and discouraged he may crave for
it; but these are his feebler moments. At his best he is self-
sufficient—content in the place of happiness with a kind of
occasional triumphant gaiety, springing from a sense of his own
fortitude and power. In the later plays which we shall examine,
we shall find Mr Shaw recognising this as fundamentally a

C

religious emotion, and trying to find the view of the universe which justifies and explains it. Meanwhile it is worth noting that the poet is the first character of this kind, who is used as a touchstone to test the metal of the others. Mr Granville Barker succeeded in playing Eugene Marchbanks where almost every other actor would have failed, because the representation of a lyrical mood is one within the peculiar range of his powers. His voice, too, can express a contemplative ecstasy. It possesses a curious individual quality, which, while it limits the range of his impersonations, gives particular intensity to some. When he repeats her name 'Candida, Candida, Candida', there is not a touch of self-consciousness in the musical reiteration; he does not appear to be following the sound of his own voice like most actors at such times, but to be listening, detached, to his longing made audible. It is in his representation of intellectual emotions that he excels, and so he excels in this part.

Miss Kate Rorke was Candida to perfection in her capacity, promptitude, width of mind and patronising kindliness; but she left out Candida's smiles, her irony, her maternity, and the *charm* of her perfect self-control. Mr C. V. France (I did not see Mr McKinnel) as James Morell did not give sufficiently the impression of a character with a large emotional surface. Morell's thoughtfulness for others, too, though it had become largely a mechanical habit, must have always had more of the natural actor's perennial impetuosity about it. Nor did Mr France give the impression of a man who is readily excited by his own words and attitudes, which Morell the orator certainly was. His performance as the parson in *The Convict on the Hearth* was a better one, though his Morell was far from being insignificant.

CANDIDA, CANDIDA, CANDIDA
February 20, 1937

CANDIDA MARKED AN important point in Mr Shaw's dramatic career. In it appeared for the first time what was to become more and more obvious, that his touchstone for the metal in human nature was an instinctive readiness in man or woman to risk happiness and be content instead with an occasional gaiety, springing from a sense of fortitude and power, and devotion to some impersonal end. As he went on, he came to identify this emotion with a religious response to life, but he seldom drama-tised it better.

The revival of *Candida* at the Globe Theatre started in me several trains of reflection, two of which are perhaps worth following up on paper. It has not been good for Bernard Shaw's art, and in the end for his 'message', that his unique position allowed him to drift so far from conventional form. The informal looseness of construction which he afterwards adopted often threw the entire onus of holding our attention on the freshness of the ideas to which his characters in turn gave utterance. In *Candida* they were embodied before our eyes in situations; *Candida*, revived, is therefore just as capable as it was thirty or thirty-five years ago of riveting us. But *Getting Married*, *Misalliance*, etc., now that the ideas debated in them are no longer startling or fresh, what chance would they have in revival? Our systems have assimilated in the course of forty years about as much Shaw, the thinker, as they will stand. We should come away from such revivals saying, 'I told you so; Shaw's a back-number'. The Globe management seems to have been afraid (quite unnecessarily) of such a verdict in the case of *Candida*. So, to liven it up with contemporary appeal, they made an awful blunder. They billed a lovely movie star in the title-role! Think of it! A faultless platinum blonde, a cynosure of cinemas, playing the part of a clever, hard-working, un-fathomably sensible wife of an East End clergyman!

This piece of miscasting made me reflect also on the difference between the technique of stage and film-acting. Between the acts I went out to look at Miss Ann Harding in her element that is to say, in a photograph, and to gaze upon her lifted chin, her perfect mouth and dreaming eyes. But on the stage she was lifeless. She moved with the gradual grace of a mermaid under water, and the expression on her face when she registered emotion (which was not often) gathered itself together so slowly that her face was often out of keeping with the words she was by that time actually uttering. She dangled her white fingers (those fingers which in the play were used to scrubbing boots, filling lamps and cutting onions) with the elegance of a Peter Lely portrait. As ill-luck would have it, she was constantly on the stage with an actress (Miss Athene Seyler) quivering with life from her tousled curls to her firm, graceless tread. I think, really, this revival ought to be renamed 'Prossy'. With one fault I have to reproach that Rejanesque comedienne who gives us so many good laughs: Miss Seyler overdoes Prossy's exit under the genial influence of champagne. I remember at the Court Theatre Miss Sydney Fairbrother got full effect out of that exit by the slight inanity of her smile at the door and just a suggestion, no more, of titubation on the way to it. It was a finer piece of work. Otherwise, Miss Seyler was wonderful.

For me Janet Achurch is still 'Candida'. The play came to Cambridge in the 'nineties while I was an undergraduate, and she was the recipient of my first bouquet (it was thus that males expressed their pleasure in those days). I was too diffident to send it round to the stage door in my own name, so I signed it 'From a Marchbanks or two', thinking there must be other admirers of eighteen in the half-empty theatre. It was Janet Achurch who revealed to me the deeper significance of the play. Marchbanks did not satisfy me till I saw the part acted by Mr Granville Barker (1904) and now he has been eclipsed—oh, yes, eclipsed—by the very remarkable performance of Mr Stephen Haggard. He is the first poet I have seen on the stage whose works I wished to read! It is worth going to the Globe Theatre simply to watch him act, though as I have said Miss Seyler is also first-rate, while Mr Nicholas Hannen gives a trenchant and vigorous version of Morell, and Mr Edward

Chapman (supplying a touch of Yorkshire) gets the fun out of the part of the egregious Mr Burgess. Mr Hannen is perhaps too rigid. He is apt, as an actor, to fall back too often on rigidity (clenched jaw and stiff posture) as means of conveying more emotion than he really expresses. There is one moment, certainly, early on in the play, where Morell should speak out of himself—and move us, when he has been goaded by Marchbanks into dropping for a moment his virile façade. It is the first time that he counters his adversary at the same depth of sincerity. I mean the line in which Morell turns on the boy crying, 'You destroy my self-confidence, and to let doubts into the citadel is devil's work'. I wanted Mr Hannen to speak that line I have paraphrased more like a man knocked out, and with an indignant helpless gesture.

JOHN BULL'S OTHER ISLAND

AT THE COURT THEATRE

November 1, 1904

IF *CANDIDA* is one of the best of Mr Shaw's plays for the completeness with which it contains and finishes its story, *John Bull's Other Island* is remarkable for being equally successful for entirely different reasons. It is a play with hardly any story, with no climax, without the vestige of a plot, and without anything like an ending, in fact without one of the qualities of the 'well-constructed' play; yet it is nevertheless an absolute success. The story is simply that of two friends and partners, an Irishman and an Englishman, who visit the former's old home in order to fore-close a mortgage. Incidentally, the Englishman determines to stand for the local seat, and becomes engaged, with his friend's approval, to a young woman with whom the latter had been on rather romantic terms for a short time before starting on his career. That is all: could anything sound more unpromising? There is not even a touch of jealousy to offer a chance for dramatic effect. The interest lies solely in the presentation of character and in the contrast between temperaments; but this is achieved in a masterly fashion. The play has the one æsthetic technical quality, which is necessary to its perfection; the characters are developed by means of a perfectly natural sequence of events; there is no appearance of circumstances being created for the sake of exhibiting them; everything that happens has the air of happening by chance.

Every critic of this play must stop on the threshold of his comments to remark, with whatever emphasis he can command, that the performance itself was one of the best ever given in

London. There were faults, of course, but they are only worth mentioning if this fact is remembered.

Mr Shaw has explained in his preface to the play what he conceives to be the main difference between the Englishman and the Irishman. The Irishman is more imaginative, but he has no illusions about matters of fact; while the Englishman is at the mercy of such imagination as he possesses, and has in consequence a confused sentimental conception of reality. The Duke of Wellington, according to him, is a typical Irishman, while Nelson is typically English. This difference in temperament he attributes not to race (he does not believe in race) but to the climate. These discussions about national characteristics make very good conversation, but it is hard to feel satisfied with their conclusions; for the exceptions are too numerous. For instance, according to Mr Shaw's theory, you would expect to find that such Englishmen as Fielding, Defoe, Cobbett, Gissing, Samuel Butler, had been brought up in the soft moist air and among the brown bogs and heather of Rosscullen, and that such Irishmen as Goldsmith and Steele, who were so full of romantic sentiment about actualities and dearly loved a fool (which Mr Shaw says is almost impossible for an Irishman) had never even been to Ireland. But whether the theory propounded in the preface is true or not, in the play Larry Doyle and Broadbent are extraordinarily vivid characters, who recall familiar types of Irishmen and Englishmen. The contrast between the two is most striking at the following points. Broadbent is full of 'heart', and takes himself and everything he does and every one he meets absolutely seriously; he has no sense of humour, or of refinement, or of proportion. Larry is discriminative to the point of chilly fastidiousness; he cannot enjoy life and he cannot idealise any human being: he cannot love, though he is fond of Tom Broadbent because Tom's warmth of emotion helps him to feel things are worth while at the moment, and because his nature is essentially practical and active, while Larry himself is capable of being moved only by ideals in which he does not believe. He is exasperated by this tendency in himself to feel only the beauty and significance of things which do not exist in any satisfying quantities; hence the bitterness of his contempt for romance and mysticism. His life is a perpetual struggle to get used to the world; it is a point of pride with him not to feel an exile here; hence his enthusiasm for the big international world of shipping, engineering and business, into which he has escaped from his dreams and thoughts in poverty-stricken Rosscullen. But business does not really fill him with enthusiasm, and he knows it; hence his fierce dislike of Father Keegan, who, with the same heart-sickness in him, has taken the opposite course, and turned away from reality to live in contemplation of a far-off perfection. Larry feels, as keenly as Father Keegan, the futility and vulgarity of Broadbent's schemes; but he fights fiercely for them because anything seems more tolerable than the helplessness of a visionary's protest against the world.

Mr J. L. Shine's Larry was not so good as many of the other parts; but he did give the impression of loneliness and distraction of heart and of perpetual tension of will to keep turned towards one path in life, which are far the most important characteristics to represent in Larry.

Broadbent, on the other hand, talks with the most reverential enthusiasm of Ruskin and Shelley (whose works he was very fond of reading, he says, as a boy), and he listens in the same spirit to the discourses of Keegan. But there is a profounder disrespect implied in his admiration than in Larry's impatience; for Broadbent is absolutely incapable of really believing in such things; the works of Ruskin and Shelley are merely pots of romantic paint to him, wherein he finds colours with which to daub his own undertakings.

Mr Louis Calvert's Broadbent was a masterpiece of acting. It is seldom that a character so thoroughly homogeneous in gesture, voice, and carriage is seen on the stage. Mr Shaw's description of him runs as follows: 'a robust, full-blooded, energetic man in the prime of life, sometimes eager and credulous, sometimes shrewd and roguish, sometimes portentously solemn, sometimes jolly and impetuous, always buoyant and irresistible, mostly likable; and enormously absurd in his most earnest moments'. Mr Calvert was all this to the life. The meeting between Broadbent and Nora Reilly by the round tower, on the first night of his arrival at Rosscullen, when his romantic feelings are so strange to himself that he accepts Nora's suggestion he is drunk, with shame and conviction, is a delicious bit of comedy. His subsequent wooing of Nora and his easy triumph offered a painful spectacle, for Nora is a charming person; but the scene is distressingly plausible.

Mr Barker as Father Keegan did not quite succeed in inspiring the sense of remote dignity which it is important to emphasise in contrast to the eupeptic irreverence of Broadbent and to the squalid go-as-you-please Irish characters. How good they all were! Corney Doyle (Mr F. Cremlin) with his drawling manner and calculating eye; Father Dempsey (Mr Beveridge) with unction, authority, and familiarity so perfectly blended in his manner; Barney Doran (Mr Wilfred Shine), the clever sloven with plenty of heartiness and no heart; and Mat Haffigan (Mr A. E. George), that gnarled old stump of dogged density! Miss Ellen O'Mally's Nora had a genuine poetic charm, a quality which hardly ever crosses the footlights.

MAN AND SUPERMAN

AT THE COURT THEATRE

1905

MAN AND SUPERMAN is one of the peaks in Bernard Shaw's dramatic work.

It was published in 1903 and first acted in 1905 at the Court Theatre under Granville Barker's direction, he taking the part of the hero, John Tanner, who was made up to look as like Shaw as possible, with a red beard and Mephistophelean eyebrows.

The play is a serio-comic love-chase of a man by a woman. But taken together with the preface, with the long dream interlude in Act III called 'Don Juan in Hell', and with its appendix, 'The Revolutionary's Handbook' (attributed to John Tanner), it remains a central exposition of Shaw's philosophy. This was the first time that his Evolutionary Religion, his conception of the Life Force as a Will striving through the minds and instincts of men to become conscious of itself, was set forth.

Yet in the play itself, with the exception of the dream interlude, there is nothing of this; and the theory which interprets sex attraction between men and women as one of the means the Life Force takes towards its end is a deduction from the play rather than a part of it. So also is the 'practical' moral that selective breeding is more important than political reforms. What does, however, pervade the dialogue and action is Shaw's conception of sex and love. In *Man and Superman*, as he says in the preface, he set out to write a play in which sex attraction should be the main subject. This, he proclaimed, no dramatist had done before. The world's famous love-tragedies and love-comedies had only dramatised conflicts, either triumphant or unhappy, between lovers and marriage laws, or love and circumstance or love and moral obligations. No dramatist, he asserted, had attempted to reveal the underlying nature of a passionate mutual attraction between a particular man and a particular woman. That startling statement had some truth in it, though all it really meant was that no dramatist had yet interpreted on the stage 'love' as the great German pessimist, Schopenhauer, had also interpreted it, namely as the Will of the Race expressing itself through the desires of the individual and often contrary to his or her happiness. Shaw also added that in love woman was really always the pursuer, and he pointed out that Shakespeare, had unconsciously, realised this in some of his plays. This theory, however, though it gains plausibility from the fact that women take love-likings as often as men, and in their own ways seek as often to win the object of their affections, cannot be accepted as sound. Still, if the case of Ann and Tanner is taken as a particular story, and not as illustrating a universal truth, this theory need not lessen our appreciation. The play is one of Shaw's most brilliant pieces of creative work.

Ann according to his philosophy is 'Everywoman', though every woman is not Ann. As an individual she is excellently drawn. Instinct leads her to mark down Tanner as the father of her future children, but Tanner knows that for him marriage means loss of liberty, peace of mind, and what is far more serious, as likely as not the ruin of his revolutionary efforts. Jack Tanner, with his explosions of nervous energy, his wit, and vehement eloquence, is as vividly created as Ann.

The contrast to him is the poetical, chivalrous, romantical Octavius, the idealiser of women who is in love with Ann. 'Ricky Ticky Tavy', as she half tenderly, half contemptuously calls him, instead of flying from her like his friend Jack Tanner, woos her humbly, but her deeper instincts—and through these, according to Shaw, the Life Force works—leads her to refuse

33

him as a husband; the poetic temperament is barren—the Life Force passes it by.

But Tanner yields at last, because, as his previous incarnation Don Juan explains in the dream episode, he cannot help it. The Life Force which wills that the offspring of two particular people shall be born, is stronger even than his impulse to serve mankind in ways to which he had intended to dedicate himself. Tanner 'loves' Ann in the sense of feeling this irresistible urge; at the same time he despises her. She is a bully and a liar and by 'unscrupulously using her personal fascinations to make men give her what she wants', she is also 'something for which there is no polite name.' He knows that she will think his aspirations and efforts to reform society absurd and thwart him in so far as she dares in the interests of the family. Above all, Ann is a hypocrite, but from an ultimate point of view that was unimportant. Both Ann and Tanner, in submitting to their attraction for each other, become servants of the will of the world. They are instruments towards creating the superior race of the future—ultimately the Superman.

Now at the time Shaw wrote this play he was evidently in a state of impatient despair in regard to what political reform could achieve. In the preface he says: 'There is no public enthusiast alive of twenty years' practical democratic experience who believes in the political adequacy of the electorate or the body it elects. The overthrow of the aristocrat has created the necessity of the Superman.' Thus both are right to sacrifice; she, perhaps her life in child-bearing, he his happiness, aims and generous ambitions; for such things cannot compare in importance with bringing into the world a child born of their mutual attraction.

It follows, of course, that the institution of marriage which compels two people who have nothing in common save mutual sex-attraction to spend their lives together, is stupid, and that from the conception that the child is the sole end of marriage, it is absurd to make it binding. Moreover, the fact that marriage is binding makes men and women who know that they will have to spend the rest of their lives together, choose their mates for irrelevant reasons—affection, respect or self-interest. That is the moral of this serio-comedy, which keeps many people laughing who would not laugh perhaps if they really understood its drift. It is rather odd that the dramatist never again returned to the theme that in selective breeding or 'eugenics', as that process is called, lay all hope of the future of mankind.

In the other characters, also, Shaw's skill in drawing types and making them speak out of themselves with arresting point is at its best. What an eye he has always had for types which were instantly recognisable and yet new to the stage or to fiction. Note here the appearance for the first time of the modern mechanician, 'Enry Straker, Tanner's chauffeur, and note too, how admirably the old-fashioned, free-thinking radical, Roebuck Ramsden, is presented, the man who can't believe that he is not still in the forefront of advanced thought, and yet is to Tanner the most ludicrous old stick-in-the-mud. The last moment of the first act, when Violet, that expertly drawn, empty-headed, possessive type of attractive girl, suddenly reveals that, instead of being the daring flaunter of conventions Tanner had hoped, she has all the time really been *married* to the man whose child she is about to bear, is one of the most amusing thunder-claps in modern comedy.

The scene at the end between Ann and Tanner, in which Ann at last gets her way, is also admirable. How it will sound on the air I cannot guess; perhaps its intensity may be lessened, when we cannot see her fainting in his arms or watch him when he declares: 'If we two now stood on the edge of a precipice I would hold you tight and jump!'

The dream-interlude, 'Don Juan in Hell', is a marvellous example of Shaw's power of making the eloquence of ideas as riveting as action on the stage. Note, by the way, his contrast between Heaven and Hell.

The point which I wish to insist upon here is not that Shaw is not right in considering his Heaven superior to his Hell—it obviously is; but that his Heaven is not the contemplation of what is perfect, but of something that is struggling to become so. It is a condition in which there is still peril, where you 'face things as they are'; in short, a 'community of saints' which is really a community of reformers. Shaw describes them as filled with 'a passion of the divine will'; but this passion is a desire to make the world better, and not a contemplation of perfection: in so far as it is a contemplative ecstasy at all, it is only rapture at the idea that perfection is possible.

What chills us, then, in his Heaven is the misgiving that the phrase 'masters of reality' (so the heavenly inhabitants are described) is a euphemism for a society of people all devoted to making each other and everybody else more virtuous. Now we can imagine something better than that; and Shaw's Hell, if he had not been so unfair to it, where they value love, music and beauty for their own sakes, offers hints at any rate.

A revised version of the original criticism, broadcast on September 16th, 1946.

YOU NEVER CAN TELL

AT THE COURT THEATRE

May 2, 1905

THE STORY OF this play is so small a part of it, that it is not worth while telling; the interest lies entirely in the characters. *You Never Can Tell* has proved one of the most popular of Mr Shaw's plays, partly because its peculiar wit and high spirits communicate to the spectator's mind a kind of dancing freedom; and partly because the criticism in it upon social distinctions, the family, and the conventions of courtship, instead of being hurled in truculent harangues across the foot-lights, is conveyed indirectly during the course of the story—and, lastly, because the whole play is tinged with the serene resignation of the old waiter's gentle refrain, 'You never can tell, sir, you never can tell.'

Connoisseurs are tiresome with their definitions of true comedy, when the upshot of them is that nothing can be comedy unless it is very like what has already been written. Mr Shaw's plays may or may not be comedy; their pervading spirit is certainly rather one of scrutiny than of indulgence, and humanity on his stage is always under the stare of a searching eye; but whether the presence of these qualities in his work settle the question or not, it is clear that *You Never Can Tell* approaches more nearly than the others to what everyone considers comedy.

How delightful is William the waiter! The 'silky old man, white-haired and delicate looking, but so cheerful and contented that in his encouraging presence ambition stands rebuked as vulgarity and imagination as treason to the abounding sufficiency and interest of the actual.' How beautifully Mr Calvert played him! He gathered the teacups with the tenderness of a lady

37

picking flowers in her garden; he proffered coats and parasols with a concern untouched by servility, but profoundly absurd; his voice was like oil on troubled waters; he was the personification of that sense of the importance of the moment, which, emphasised, is the source of the most delicious irony. What a dissertation might be written upon William! William the leveller, William the impassive, William the imperturbably, universally kind! His kinship might be shown to the overarching blue, which dwarfs frantic gesticulations and is no sounding-board for violent declaimers. One cannot help regretting that his spirit does not more often brood over the plays of Mr Shaw.

The love interest in this play has already been discussed in connection with Mr Shaw's general treatment of that theme; but it is worth while insisting again upon its main feature. Love appears as an impulse which cannot be rationalised, only explained. The state of falling in love is, according to this theory, one that a clear-headed man will recognise as a kind of dream, in which individuals have a value his wide-awake judgment would never allow them. That is to say, it makes complete nonsense of life. In his later plays Mr Shaw justifies it on the ground of a faith in the purposes of nature, of 'the Life Force'; in this one, Valentine, unlike Tanner who philosophises upon it, recklessly enjoys its exhilaration, though he knows it may land him where he has no wish to be. When Gloria, like Ann, turns round to hold her lover, who when it comes to the point would be half glad to get off, it is curious to note that the audience always roars with laughter, just as they did at the tremendous moment in the last act of *Man and Superman*. If this jars on those who see the serious intention of the author, how trying it must be to the actors themselves.

The Twins, who are so delightful to the reader, never quite came up to expectation on the stage. High spirits and spontaneous fun are extraordinarily difficult to act; especially when they take the form of a burlesque of sententiousness.

The Twins are always acting up to a comic conception of themselves; it is very hard for actors to represent two young creatures doing this *naturally*. The fault I had to find with the playing of Miss Dorothy Minto and Mr Page is that they did not exhibit constantly enough the physical signs of those animal spirits which prompt their irrepressible comments. The rollicking tirades about their twentieth-century mother and Gloria, in the first act, did not quite come off for this reason. In Miss Minto, who was admirable in the quarrel with her father, I missed the flash of teeth and eyes in smiling, which I imagine to have been one of the characteristics which made the assaults of the real Dolly flabbergasting; but when she was momentarily suppressed she was excellent. Mr Page lacked vivacity. But certainly this want is better than the overacting the part so easily invites.

Miss Watson brought out the women's rights side of Mrs. Clandon. You could imagine how carefully just she always tried to be to her children; but you missed the indulgent maternal quality in her, which was so remarkable in Mrs Wright's impersonation, making the family much more conceivable as a family, and Mrs. Clandon's implacable attitude to her husband much more interesting. Owing to this defect in Miss Watson's finished acting, the scene in which the Twins, after trying to get out of their mother the name of their father, go over to her side against Gloria, did not seem significant.

Mr Edmund Gurney, as Crampton, cut as unamiably grotesque a figure as he ought. He was wonderfully unattractive, and, when he climbed down and dropped the domineering father, like all unattractive cross-grained people trying to conciliate affection, he became pitiable. There was real pathos in the pleading glances of his dazed and choleric little eye, in the movements of his mouth, as though he found consideration for others a bitter draught, and in the clumsy, checked gestures of his tenderness. Mr James Hearn as Bohun used a fine hectoring voice; but he emphasised the already too frequent

39

repetitions in his part by a monotonous shaking of his finger at the individual to be put down.

The part of Valentine was played on different occasions by Mr Granville Barker and Mr Ainley. The latter's was a very fair performance, but he did not convey well the gaiety and violence of Valentine's character. Where Mr Barker excelled was precisely in those brisk leaps of the heart, which are so characteristic of Mr Shaw's lovers; for instance, in such a passage as this, at the end of an interview during which Gloria has been very scornful, he was superb.

> VALENTINE. Love can't give any man new gifts. It can only heighten the gifts he was born with.
> GLORIA. What gifts were you born with, pray?
> VALENTINE. Lightness of heart.
> GLORIA. And lightness of head and lightness of faith, and lightness of everything that makes a man.
> VALENTINE. Yes, the whole world is like a feather dancing in the light now, and Gloria is the sun. I beg your pardon; I'm off. Back at nine. Good-bye.

Mr Barnes' Finch McComas was a most delightful piece of comedy. Finch in his youth was an ardent reformer; when he appears on the stage he is an eminently respectable solicitor. His character bears some analogy to Roebuck Ramsden; they are both 1870 types, only Finch is well aware that his ideas are no longer advanced. He informs Mrs Clandon, newly arrived from Madeira, that the ideas they upheld together in their youth, for which she is still strenuously prepared to suffer social ostracism, are now perfectly respectable; in fact, that they might be professed by any bishop. Only in one place could they possibly be considered as advanced—in the theatre.

AT THE EVERYMAN

February 26, 1921

AT THE EVERYMAN THEATRE, Hampstead, a 'Shaw Season' is running. The company has just finished playing *You Never*

Can Tell. The atmosphere of this little theatre (by its atmosphere I mean the spirit which animates actors and audience) is not unlike that in which Mr Shaw's early plays were first produced. Of course, we had not the other night the ardour of those early audiences, who believed (quite rightly) that they were hailing an original and important dramatist; neither was there, I expect, one person among us who was puzzled or outraged by the behaviour of the characters and the sentiments expressed. The young, I understand, consider it a mark of fogeyism to admire Mr Shaw seriously. Seen from their angle he is that most pathetic of figures, the old pioneer. But I am not personally much interested in the shifting meanings of the word 'advanced'. What interested me in this revival of *You Never Can Tell* was the degree to which the originality of the play in spite of being so familiar made itself felt. What gave me pleasure was the invention shown in the situations and the clear-cut way character was presented. Yes, the play and the humour were still fresh; originality 'keeps'. The only passage which dated was Finch's remark to Mrs Clandon who, revisiting England after many years, still supposes that her ideas, those of a free-thinking individualist of the 'seventies and 'eighties, would still shock people. Finch informs her that there is only one place where her views will be considered outrageous. 'The Church?' she suggests at once. 'No', he replies, 'the Theatre.' I remember the roar of laughter which greeted that remark when it was first heard. The other night it was received in silence, not because it has not still a sting of truth in it, but because, thanks chiefly to Mr Shaw himself, the criticism has become a commonplace.

Miss Massingham in some respects satisfied me more than any Gloria I have seen. She brought out the priggish side of her so well, the ungraciousness of her tenderness, and her final determination to swallow her humiliation and to grab what she wants. These characteristics are easier for a younger generation to grasp. On the other hand, the pathos of Gloria's bewilderment, of her momentary agonised collapse into her mother's arms, and her earlier easy confidence, that attractive consciousness of her own charms, slowly smiling and gay, proper to the unapproachable belle of Madeira, she did not convey so well. Mr Hannen was a painstaking Valentine. At first I thought I was not going to like him at all, but after a time he ingratiated himself. But where were the high dancing spirits? His Valentine was not a man capable of Valentine's quick fantastic adroitness, still less of that towering scene with Gloria which always strikes me as one of the best love-scenes in modern comedy.

The Twins—I have never seen the twins done to perfection. Mr Banks buffooned it too self-consciously; Miss Hazel Jones was too minxish. The twins are very difficult to act because they are conscious of themselves as comic characters and behave accordingly; yet it is of the first importance they should suggest that they are the reverse of self-conscious. The element they contribute (not counting fun) to the comedy is the innocent hardness and delicious inconsiderateness of youth, but their hardness must be innocent, their inconsiderateness charming, or we lose the pathos, and it is real pathos, of Dolly getting up suddenly from the lunch table, shocked and surprised to tears, when her father is violently rude to her. Otherwise, too, we lose the seriousness of that important second when the boy looks back into the room before following his old father to the dance—poor Crampton has asked for a false nose and mask in the hopeless hope of getting into touch with his children—'Mother', Philip says, 'do you observe the pathos of that?' It is a gleam of comprehension—perfectly natural, just right. The next minute the boy will forget all about it. The hardness and directness of youth and the softness of old age, with its need for consideration, is a theme Mr Shaw has dealt with more directly in *Misalliance*. He understands it in all its bearings very well. Youth, without thinking, instinctively feels it has the whip-hand, and Age in spite of formidable bluster, knows that Youth has it. Am I attributing a non-existent blindness to the public, or is it still necessary to write about 'The Subtlety of Bernard Shaw'?

Miss Margaret Carter's Mrs Clandon was a charming performance. The generous, indulgent side of her character was well brought out, which is so important in making the family interesting and the twins plausible. On the other hand, her bland, platform, eminent-woman side was not shown. It is impossible to fail in the part of William the waiter, but Mr Brember Wills irritated me a little by emphasising the *can* in the refrain 'You never can tell'.

MAJOR BARBARA

AT THE COURT THEATRE

November 28, 1905

MAJOR BARBARA is the story of a woman who lives her religion and loses it; who, after enduring the desolation of seeing her own and all the world's hope hang torn before her eyes, finds at last a belief her passionate heart can live by. This account will seem ridiculous to those who heard only the crackle of wit, the rhetoric of theory, and brisk interchange of comment; yet it is the centre and significance of the play.

It is the first English play which has for its theme the struggle between two religions in one mind. And to have written upon that theme convincingly is a triumph which criticism cannot appreciably lessen. The second act is 'wonderful, most wonderful, and yet again wonderful, and after that past all whooping'.

Barbara is the daughter of the chief partner in the biggest cannon-manufactory in the world. Her mother is a lady of birth and position, 'well mannered yet appallingly outspoken and indifferent to the opinions of her interlocutors, arbitrary and high-tempered to the last bearable degree, full of class prejudices, conceiving the universe exactly as if it were a large house in Wilton Crescent, though handling her corner of it very effectively on that assumption'. Barbara's parents have been living apart for years.

When the play begins, the engagement of Lady Britomart's two daughters to young men without money has compelled her to ask her husband to call upon her in order that she may persuade him to make a fitting provision for them. The one daughter is a very ordinary society girl; the other, Barbara has a genius for saving souls, and is already a prominent officer in the Salvation Army. She is engaged to Cusins, a professor of Greek, who fell in love with her and proposed under the impression that she was an ordinary Salvation Army lass.

The first act introduces these people, and its interest lies in the return of Undershaft to the bosom of his family. Lady Britomart was admirably played by Miss Filippi. On Undershaft's being announced I had a vivid recollection of her adjusting her spectacles and settling herself in a chair facing the door with an admirable air of nervous decision. Mr Calvert's Undershaft was not nearly so good as his blusterous Broadbent or his balmy 'William'; for Undershaft is good-natured and easy-going on the surface but fuliginous and formidable underneath, but Mr Calvert was complacent underneath and formidable on the surface. Of all Undershaft's family Barbara alone interests him, and his heart goes out to her, though he would resent such a description of his feelings. They both have religious natures, but the beliefs of each are poles asunder. Each wishes to convert the other, and they strike a bargain; he will visit her Salvation Army shelter, if she will afterwards visit his gun-manufactory. The second act is laid at the shelter.

There is no space in which to dilate upon the pathos, passion, and significant realism of this scene, or upon the ironic ecstasy which Cusins contributes to it (imagine the difficulty of acting such a purely intellectual passion!); but one incident must be noted. Bill Walker, a bullying sort of ruffian, slouches in to recover 'his girl', who has been recently converted; and when one of the Salvation lasses tells him she has gone away, he hits her in the mouth. Now, this blow very nearly brings about his own conversion; for Jenny Hill does not resent it, and Major Barbara takes advantage of the shame which begins to stir in him to make him more and more uncomfortable. His impulse is to buy back his peace of mind and self-respect by getting thrashed by his girl's new Salvation Army 'bloke', and failing in this, he offers Jenny a sovereign. Barbara tells him he cannot buy his salvation; she wants to touch his heart, and if he were to think he had made amends, he would go away as stupid and brutal as he came. Her father all the while watches this soul-saving process with grim sympathy. His chance comes when the news arrives that Bodger, the whisky-distiller, has offered a £5,000 subscription if another £5,000 can be raised. The money is of vital importance to the Army; indeed this shelter will have to be closed if funds are not forthcoming. Barbara has already refused £100 from her father for the same reason that she refused Bill's twenty shillings—because she wants her father to give up manufacturing the means of death; and if he can ease his conscience by being charitable, he will go on making money out of the sufferings of men. But the Army does not attach so much importance to the saving of Undershaft's soul as to the power his money will give them to help many others; so when he offers to make up the other £5,000 they accept it with grateful thanksgivings and Hallelujahs. This is a terrible shock to Barbara, who realises, for the first time, that the power of the Army rests ultimately on the support of its worst enemies, who make the money they give away out of the very misery and degradation which the Army fights. The other side to this view is put by Mrs Baines: 'Who would have thought that any good could have come out of war and drink? And yet their profits are brought to-day to the feet of salvation to do its blessed work.' Barbara sees that Bodger 'wants to send his cheque down to buy us and go on being as wicked as ever'; while Cusins exclaims with excited irony, 'The millennium will be inaugurated by the unselfishness of Undershaft and Bodger. O be joyful!' The Army must accept the money, since they are powerless without it; but the fact that they are right to accept it shows that they are fighting a battle they can never win; since if once they begin to make real headway against Bodger, his subscriptions, which are their means of victory, will be cut off. Barbara realises this on reflection; but at the moment it is the revelation of the spring whence the Army's power is drawn, coupled with the object lesson that the Army cannot afford to think of the individual soul while such supplies are in question, which tumbles her faith to the ground. She is quite certain that a crusade which draws its strength from the evils it wishes to destroy, cannot put the world straight. This is a criticism which hits all the churches and all charitable institutions in so far as they hope to do this. From a revolutionist's point of view, they are also objectionable, because they tend to keep the poor quiet, by making them less discontented with conditions which they ought to die rather than stand, and the rich from thinking they are just and honest, by offering them opportunities of being generous and kind; in short, because they keep those who should be indignant, servile, and those who ought to be uneasy, self-satisfied.

Undershaft's gospel, on its social side, is to preach socialism to the rich and rebellion to the poor, whereby he twists the same rope from both ends. The most important fact to insist upon is, therefore, the importance of money; tacitly, this is recognised by everyone; the possession of comfortable independence being everywhere the most universally powerful motive. But instead of blinking this fact and preaching 'Blessed are the poor', while taking care at the same time to have a reliable source of income ourselves, we must preach 'Cursed be the poor', so that every poverty-stricken man may either feel he has a grievance not to be borne, or be ashamed of the feebleness which keeps him so. The way in which Undershaft puts it is that poverty is literally *the worst of crimes*, and it follows from this assertion that a man is right to commit any other crime to avoid that one, should circumstances force him into such a dilemma. Now this is a doctrine that good sense refuses to swallow. How then did Undershaft or Mr Shaw come to believe it, and urge it with such vehemence?

The temperament and interests of a reformer drive him to look continually at results of actions and emotions in valuing them rather than at these things themselves; and since poverty and ill-health are probably the causes of more evil than is any single vice, the reformer slips more readily than other people into the mistake of thinking that these things are, in themselves, worse than any vice. But it is clear that what may be a cause of evil is often not even bad at all in itself, let alone not so bad as the evil; and equally, that the means to good are often valueless in themselves, compared to what they help to bring about. That poverty is not bad in itself—is no more a crime than is a broken leg—is so clear that if a man of Mr Shaw's talents had not said it was, no critic would bore his reader with a refutation of such a statement. Bunyan and Blake, whom Mr Shaw praises with such liberality of genuine admiration, were very poor; yet that they were among the most ignoble of criminals he himself would never admit.

It is clear that poverty, like ill-health, is only bad as a difficulty in the way of a fine life which a few surmount, and that therefore the pretext of escaping from it cannot justify the worst actions. Indeed, if Undershaft's doctrine were generally believed, the only effect would be to make poverty the cause of much more evil, of many more acts of violence, oppression and meanness, than it is now. Dubedat took every means in his power—blackmailing, stealing, utilising his wife's charms as bait—to escape poverty; yet I do not think Undershaft would have felt that he was doing much to bring about a better state of things.

And Undershaft himself? He talks very big about having been prepared to kill anybody as long as he was poor; but what did he *do*? Did he found his fortunes by knocking an old woman on the head and stealing her watch, or by going into partnership with a Mrs Warren? No, of course not; he stuck to his desk like a good young man, inched and pinched until he had made himself useful to the firm, and then took good care not to be put upon. Undershaft's weakness lay in talking big; that is really what his sensible wife could not stand. In

Act II he tells his son that he and Lazarus are really the people who govern England, and decide questions of war and peace; and in Act III he explains to Cusins that he is a fool if he accepts the partnership in the hope of power, since he and Lazarus are in fact absolutely powerless. In both cases he is talking big.

In this third and last act Barbara and her family visit the town of Perivale St. Andrews. They find it is a clean, fine place, where everybody is well-fed and well-clad. It is, in fact, a kind of socialistic community with this great difference; instead of being pervaded with a spirit of equality and independence, the whole place is honey-combed with snobbishness and petty oppression. This spirit is what Barbara will spend her life now in fighting. Her work will be amongst uppish, vulgar, prosperous, self-satisfied people, and her last speech is a pæan of rejoicing that she will in future never feel the humiliation of knowing that the truths she has at heart are listened to because she distributes alms at the same time.

The last act is weak on the stage; indeed the defect of the play is that Barbara's conversion is much less impressive than the loss of her old religion. Miss Annie Russell, who was so good in the first two acts, could make little of the third.

The moral of the play filtered from Undershaft's plutocratic gospel would run as follows: that the ideal state is one in which no one is poor; that the ideal man is he who shifts vigorously for himself; that the best cure for the present anarchic and miserable state of things, is that every individual should become self-reliant and use the weapons which Undershaft manufactures against those who oppress him; that those who have already some wealth and independence are the people it is most profitable to teach what is good; that to the rest it is more important to preach rebellion. If *Man and Superman* is in a sense the cry of reformer clinging to the idea of selective breeding of mankind in the wreck of his hopes, *Major Barbara* expresses the disappointed impatience of a pamphleteer who gives up his belief in persuasion and turns to the swifter agency of force. The fallacy which the play attacks with perfect justice, is that of preaching to or of helping the poor simply because they are *poor*.

The mistake into which Mr Shaw slips of saying that poverty is a crime far worse than murder or lust or avarice, since it is perhaps a more constant *cause* of crime and feebleness than any one of these, is a fallacy which in one form or other often occurs in his writings. His great defect as an artist-philosopher is that he does not distinguish between those things which are bad as means and those which are bad in themselves, or between what is good as an end and what is only good as a means to that end; that when he judges the actions and emotions or the lives and characters of men and women, his test is invariably— What use are they? If he feels them to be useful as a means to reforming society, then they are good; if they cannot be shown to be useful, or only to be less useful than something else, then they are judged to be comparatively valueless. But it is certain that qualities and things which are valuable as means are not necessarily worth having for their own sakes, and that things very good in themselves may not at the same time be important as means to something else worth having. And since this is indubitably true, it follows that any one who judges the values of things from the point of view of their results, and hardly ever asks himself whether they have any value in themselves, must often get his scale of values wrong. This is the most general criticism which can be brought against the morality of the Shavian drama. A great part of that originality of view which underlies the plays is due to the fact that he judges goodness and badness by their results alone. The transvaluation which follows is often startling; actions which nobody thought particularly bad are put in a class with the most heinous offences, and qualities not commonly allowed to be claims upon the respect of others are exalted above affection. In this he is often right, because the goodness of things as a means may be an important part of their total value; but he is, also, often wrong, because the importance of anything as a means to something else may be a very small part of its total value. For instance, what are the qualities most extolled in his plays? Vitality, pugnacity, political and intellectual honesty, fearlessness and universal benevolence: these are clearly useful. What are the qualities and emotions which on the whole are depreciated or pointedly ignored? Personal affections, admiration, and sensitiveness to beauty: these cannot be shown to be such powerful means towards bringing about a better state of society; but are they not essential elements in that better state itself? Mr Shaw ignores the question of ultimate ends so completely that when he defines Heaven, the ideal state, he describes it as a community of men working towards bringing it into existence. 'In Heaven you live and work, instead of playing and pretending, you face things as they are; you escape nothing but glamour, and your steadfastness and your peril are your glory. . . . But even as you [the devil] enjoy the contemplation of such romantic mirages as beauty and pleasure, so would I enjoy the contemplation of that which interests me above all things: namely, Life: the force that ever strives to attain greater power of contemplating itself.' Hell is a community in which personal relations and the contemplation of beauty are the supreme goods. Mr Shaw cheapens this ideal by assuming that the only kind of love which can compete with the fellow-service of heaven is a kind which might be worthily sung by Sedley, or set to music by Offenbach, or depicted by Fragonard. No one requires to be told that Mohammed's paradise, however intellectualised and refined, is not the highest good; but what is instructive in Mr Shaw's antithesis is that he sets so much store by the contemplation of what is both real and beautiful at the same time, raising this above the contemplation of beauty or goodness which is not accompanied by a true belief in the object. That this judgment is a true one nobody can doubt; what can be protested against with equal justice is the assumption that love between individuals always implies contemplation of goodness and beauty which cannot be believed to be real.

December 2, 1905

IT WOULD REQUIRE four articles to criticise *Major Barbara* fairly; one to describe what we felt as we watched the play; one to say what we thought when the tide of emotion had gone out and we could examine calmly the wrinkles which the waves had left in the sand; another to praise the excellence of the acting, which was worth the attention of the most discriminating amateur; and lastly, an article, which should take the form of an extra Christmas number, to analyse with seasonable charity and exhilaration the coherence of Mr Shaw's philosophy. But dramatic criticism has its 'form', alas, like other methods of expression, and 'to be continued in our next' is forbidden by it. We must content ourselves, therefore, and attempt to content our readers, by cramming the harvest of a critic's eye into the columnal sack.

We are bound to say that our impression of *Major Barbara* was that it is one of the most remarkable plays put upon the English stage; and for this reason: it is the first play in which the religious passion has been really presented. Religion and Love are the most interesting of all human passions. They are so interesting that any book or any play which shows, truthfully, how any kind of man, however negligible in other respects, is affected by them, even if it only shows how little he is affected by them, becomes itself wonderfully interesting. Where love is concerned he may be mad with much heart or idiot with none; if a writer can really show what the character in question felt and the true value of his feelings, his book is worthy to be printed on vellum and kept in a fireproof library from generation to generation. Where religion is concerned, in the sense of what a man really feels about his destiny and his duty, the same holds good. His conception of what he believes may be very different from what he actually does believe. He may consider himself an atheist and be religious, like Shelley, or think himself orthodox and pious, and unconsciously refer all his judgment and actions to principles which contradict his creed, like a bellicose bishop, or he may 'care for none of these things'. It does not matter; if the author can only draw such an attitude towards life as it is, he will have written a book or play of real importance. The greater part of Mr Shaw's work consists in showing, with wit and vigour and courage, the difference between what people feel and what they think they feel; the latter is usually decided by what they think they *ought* to feel. There are clamours about his cynicism in consequence. Had he not the jester's privilege of saying what is in his mind and the jester's disability of being ignored when it is convenient, he would be well hated. But this great merit of his work is lessened by a superstition. Numerous utterances of his give us the impression that he believes that what a man feels, without reflection or reference to principle, is always the right judgment, and what he thinks he *ought* to feel is always the wrong one; that it is always 'conscience' which makes fools of us all; that self-assertion and grabbing what you want are the only true instincts; and that to entertain the notion that your motives may be more complicated is the sign of incomplete self-knowledge. It is true that wrong things are often done from conscientious motives, but is there any other truth in this Rousseau-like superstition? When a character, through whom Mr Shaw ventriloquises, such as Tanner or Undershaft, is tackled by another person in the play, he usually takes refuge in the assertion that 'good' is an inapplicable adjective and corresponds to no real quality in men or actions; an assertion which he naturally has to forget before launching upon his next moral tirade. His leading characters are always men and women of almost hypertrophied conscientiousness. This is the reason his writings are so confusing. Each point is made so clearly that the audience think they must either be fools not to carry away the gist of the whole play in a nutshell, or that Mr Shaw has been leading them purposely a jack-o'-lantern dance. Patients under anæsthetics have described a sensation of being on the verge of discovering the meaning of the universe; the more sympathetic among Mr Shaw's audiences are continually enraptured by a very similar sensation. The argumentative contentions are so spirited and direct that you expect every moment a new and permanent illumination to burst upon your mind. But when the play is over, the resulting idea is often hardly more applicable as an explanation than the perception which a philosopher is said to have recorded on recovering consciousness from chloroform, 'a strong smell of turpentine pervades the whole'. This confusion and disappointment is due, firstly, to the fact that his mouthpiece characters first repudiate the idea that any moral perception can possibly be true, and then proceed to propound a system of their own; and, secondly, because they judge the value of every emotion and action by its results alone, never considering whether it has any value in itself or not.

So, too, nothing is bad if it produces incidentally any good results whatever; neither murder, nor hatred, nor lust, nor lying. Nor, again, apparently, is anything good, neither love, nor compassion, nor beauty, for these cannot always be shown to lead directly to the reformation of society, a reformation (and here is the confusing circle) which can, as a matter of fact, only consist in bringing more of such good things into existence. Why miscall these excellent things because, as yet, they are found only here and there in the world? What else is there to aim at except these things which Mr Shaw's reformers brush aside as worthless? It surely stares every man in the face, that what is worth having in itself is not always the most efficient means to something else worth having, and that such means often have little or no value in themselves. Why deny it? Mr Shaw is a writer of genius and cannot help reflecting life as he sees it in spite of his theories. His characters are never quite fined into incarnations of a philosophic point. Though he seems often to try his best to whittle them down to that, they nearly always escape from his hands. Undershaft, for instance, consistently repudiates the idea that he wants his children's love; he will only accept their respect; but he becomes alive and interesting through the attraction which draws him to his daughter Barbara. In Mr Shaw's work we have a very real picture of life, but it is scored with the incessant and authoritative commentaries of a circular philosophy. No wonder we do not know, half the time, whether we are on our heads or on our heels. Notwithstanding, *Major Barbara* is a noble story, real as life. But why did the author trick out and overlay his theme with trifling diversions? The comedy of ordinary life was necessary as a contrast to show the incongruity of surroundings in which such things happen—namely, among relations and friends, who, intent on their own concerns, remain almost perfectly indifferent; but why dazzle the audience with fireworks till it grows blind to the real point?

Much talk about life was necessary to explain the difference between Barbara's old religion and her new; but why fill the speeches with explanations addressed more to the audience than to Barbara? For though these interest some, they bore others, and they would certainly have been equally effective if read in a book. But Mr Shaw has written the first play with religious passion for its theme and has made it real. That is a triumph no criticisms can lessen. Barbara first lives in the religion of pity and humility, typified by the Salvation Army, which tries to save the world by spiritual methods alone. Then she finds that the influence of these methods depends ultimately upon the support of its enemies, of those whose fortunes are made out of the very miseries she tries to cure. The work under her supervision must slacken, the shelters must be closed, unless money is subscribed by liquor manufacturers and by such men as her father. It is their interest to encourage the palliatives of charity and religion; since it keeps discontent from becoming dangerous. She will not be bought; but the institution she belongs to clutches eagerly at the money, so she leaves it and relinquishes her belief in a God of mercy and humility: he cannot save the world. Then she begins to listen to the religion of her father. His is the religion of pride and self-reliance, of which the first commandment is, be strong, and therefore rich; since force decides at last what kind of men will shape the world in their own image. He has two mottoes, 'unashamed', and 'Nothing is ever done, until men are prepared to kill one another unless it is done'—a motto which has much support in history. Therefore, to help men you must make them first easy and healthy; afterwards they will have strength and pride enough to demand what belongs to them by right. She accepts her father's fortune that she may get her hands upon the gear of the world, and her last speech is the pæan of her new religion.

'I have got rid of the bribe of bread. I have got rid of the bribe of heaven. When I die let Him be in my debt, not I in His. Let God's will be done for its own sake. The work that He created us to do can only be done by *living* men and women.' This fine speech comes at the end of other speeches, emphatic and long, and therefore it is impossible for any actress to give it its full effect, for the audience has listened already to too many torrents of words.

Here, then, is fought out to an issue, in the heart of a living being, the struggle between two active religions. The one does not feel dirt, misery, and helplessness to be utterly intolerable, since a soul may often be easier 'to save' in such a plight; while the other asserts that justice is the first debt owing from man to man, and that until that has been paid no one who is honest can offer anything else to the unfortunate.

CAPTAIN BRASSBOUND'S CONVERSION

AT THE COURT THEATRE

March 20, 1906

THE MORAL OF this play is that revenge is silly and vulgar, and justice with retaliatory punishments is only a wilder kind of revenge. Lady Cecily Waynflete manages and keeps in perfect order the horde of ramshackle banditti, amongst whom she and her brother find themselves, by ignoring their dangerous intentions as childish naughtinesses, and treating every one of them as though they were amiable fellows. Her power springs from absolute fearlessness and a most kindly sympathy, which is not in her an irregular or interrupted impulse, but a constant feeling. She is a gentle, humorous, cheerful, naturally domesticated person, but a very persistent immovable one. To borrow a metaphor, there is in her nature a quality which answers to the fly-wheel in a mill, which distributes the motion equably over all the wheels. She is always telling people what pleasant faces they have and how much she likes them; and this is how she genuinely feels towards all she meets. The story runs as follows: Sir Howard Hallam, one of His Majesty's judges, and Lady Cecily, his sister-in-law, are taking a holiday tour in Morocco. They are anxious to make an expedition into the interior, a tract of country which is dangerous to Christian travellers, owing to the fanaticism of the Mohammedan tribes. A certain Captain Brassbound, who carries on a dubious coasting trade (really smuggling and piracy), sometimes provides an escort for tourists in this district. In spite of the warnings of the missionary at the coast town, they determine to trust him; though Lady Cecily is, of course, reluctant to have an escort at all; such men, she says, always want such a lot of looking after. However, Sir Howard and the missionary are firm on this point, and she resigns herself. She is not the least alarmed when she hears that every native believes that he will go to heaven if he kills an unbeliever, and replies with point, 'Bless you, dear Mr Rankin, the people in England believe that they will go to heaven if they give all their property to the poor. But they don't do it. I'm not a bit afraid of that.'

Now Brassbound is really the son of Sir Howard's brother. His mother was a drunken half-crazy woman, who after her husband's death pestered the judge, her brother-in-law, to such an extent that he had an order of restraint made out against her. There was a piece of property, too, in Jamaica, over which there was a long legal dispute; it is now in the judge's hands. The upshot of all this, as far as concerns the position of the characters at the beginning of the play, is that Captain Brassbound, alias 'Black Paquito', has been nursing for years a romantic hatred of his uncle, as the murderer and robber of his mother; Sir Howard, of course, never dreams of the relationship between them. It is the captain's intention to revenge his mother by delivering the travellers over to the mercy of the fanatic, Sidi el Assif. But his whole romantic scheme of revenge collapses on closer acquaintance with Lady Cecily. He clings to it desperately because he has invested all his self-respect in the idea that he is a wronged man, who has a great act of reparative justice to perform; but it is no use; her kindliness, perfect good faith, and good sense, take the life out of this revenge. He begins by resenting and repulsing her kind actions towards himself and his men; but these are so practical, and are done in so amiable a spirit that he cannot hold out long. There is an explosive scene, of course, between Captain Brassbound and Sir Howard, when the former declares his relationship and resolve, in which Sir Howard speaks up stoutly, declaring that Brassbound may do his worst, but that he and the rest of his gang shall certainly swing for it, while Lady Cecily sits by rather distressed, but quite calm. After this scene follows a dialogue between her and Captain Brassbound, so typical of the delightful serious comedy of the whole play that it must be quoted.

BRASSBOUND. Don't quibble with me. I am going to do my duty as a son; and you know it.

LADY CECILY. But I should have thought the time for that was in your mother's lifetime, when you could have been kind and forbearing with her. Hurting your uncle won't do her any good, you know.

BRASSBOUND. It will teach other scoundrels to respect widows and orphans. Do you forget that there is such a thing as justice?

LADY CECILY [*gaily shaking out the finished coat*]. Oh, if you are going to dress yourself in ermine and call yourself Justice, I give you up. You are just your uncle over again; only he gets £5,000 a year for it, and you do it for nothing. [*She holds the coat up to see if any further repairs are needed.*]

BRASSBOUND [*sulkily*] You twist my words very cleverly. But no man or woman has ever changed me.

LADY CECILY. Dear me! That must be very nice for the people you deal with, because they can always depend on you; but isn't it rather inconvenient for yourself when you change your mind?

BRASSBOUND. I never change my mind.

LADY CECILY [*rising with the coat in her hands*]. Oh! oh! Nothing will ever persuade me that you are as pigheaded as that.

BRASSBOUND [*offended*]. Pigheaded!

LADY CECILY [*with quick, caressing apology*]. No, no, no. I didn't mean that. Firm! Unalterable! Resolute! Ironwilled. Stonewall Jackson. That's the idea, isn't it?

BRASSBOUND [*hopelessly*] You are laughing at me.

LADY CECILY. No. Trembling, I assure you. Now will you try this on for me? I'm so afraid I have made it too tight under the arm. [*She holds it behind him.*]

BRASSBOUND [*obeying mechanically*]. You take me for a fool, I think. [*He misses the sleeve.*]

LADY CECILY. No; all men look foolish when they are feeling for their sleeves—

59

BRASSBOUND. Agh! [*He turns and snatches the coat from her; then puts it on himself and buttons the lowest button.*]

LADY CECILY [*horrified*]. Stop. No, you must never pull a coat at the skirts, Captain Brassbound; it spoils the sit of it. Allow me. [*She pulls the lapels of his coat vigorously forward.*] Put back your shoulders. [*He frowns but obeys.*] That's better. [*She buttons the top button.*] Now button the rest, from the top down. Does it catch you at all under the arm?

BRASSBOUND [*miserably—all resistance beaten out of him*]. No.

LADY CECILY. That's right. Now, before I go back to poor Marzo, say thank you to me for mending your jacket, like a nice polite sailor.

BRASSBOUND [*sitting down at the table in great agitation*]. Damn you! You have belittled my whole life to me. [*He bows his head on his hands, convulsed.*]

LADY CECILY [*quite understanding, and putting her hand kindly on his shoulder*]. Oh no. I am sure you have done lots of kind things and brave things, if you could only recollect them. With Gordon, for instance? Nobody can belittle that.

But the Sidi is on his way, and Captain Brassbound cannot now prevent his vengeance working itself out. However, an American gun-boat has been warned to keep an eye on the fate of the travellers, and by firing a few guns they succeed in frightening off the fanatics, and Captain Brassbound and his crew are marched off in custody.

The last act is delightful; in it the Captain, dressed by Lady Cecily's orders in her brother's, the ambassador's, top hat and frock coat, looking appallingly stiff and grotesquely smart, comes up for court-martial with his crew. Lady Cecily explains everything away; how the two quarrelled when they found they were related, how well Captain Brassbound behaved; in short, she garbles the events in the most exquisitely ingenious fashion. Of course they are all acquitted. The play ends with Brassbound asking Lady Cecily what he is to do now, since she has knocked the bottom out of his old life. He blurts out a proposal of marriage, and she is almost hypnotised into saying yes; but the signal-gun breaks the spell, and he returns to his ship, glad that he has not persuaded her to sacrifice herself, and confident that he knows what is the secret of influence over men at last—disinterested, fearless sympathy.

The rare merit of the play lies in making you think most seriously of the relations of men to each other and laugh at the same time. Since Swift no such insistent preacher has so leavened his lesson with laughter. Dickens both preached and laughed, but he stopped laughing the moment he began to preach.

The humour in this play hovers perpetually on the edge of that tender emotion which the sight of great kindness and reasonableness stirs. Nowhere else, except in the second act of *Major Barbara*, is Mr Shaw's emotional asceticism so perfectly justified by the results. This distrust of the melting mood is one of his most marked characteristics as a writer, and in a hortatory artist it is a sound instinct. For although men in a softened mood may take a deep impression more easily, such an impression is not likely to recur to them so often afterwards as those received at other times. The reformer does well, in conveying his moral, to aim at creating a mood which is more like those in which men ordinarily make their decisions. One reason why exciting harangues, whether moral or religious or political, influence so little the conduct of men who have nevertheless been deeply moved by them, is that the mood in which they felt the significance of what was said is one which normal circumstances rarely arouse again; the orator has 'taken them out of themselves;' but the truth perceived when 'they were themselves' is never quite forgotten.

The Court Theatre performance was below the usual mark, and not so good as that which the Stage Society gave some years before. It lacked those qualities of proportion and completeness which they have attained in almost every other case. The cast did not pull the play well together. Miss Ellen Terry contributed some delightful touches to the character of

Lady Cecily, and all her own charm; but there was a hesitation in her acting sometimes, which robbed it of effect.*

Mr Frederick Kerr, as Brassbound, was not violent and dangerous enough. His attitudes and voice suggested an underlying fund of good nature, which detracts from the impressiveness of Lady Cecily's imperturbable serenity and her conquest of him. His 'grrr-s' were guttural enough; but not sufficiently ferocious. It is important that he should behave with great brutality to her in the second act; so that the reaction of compunction, when he is finally overcome by her sweetness and kind good sense, may seem more significant and moving. Mr Gwenn as Drinkwater was clever; but far too exaggerated; especially when he begs that his penny shockers may be returned to him. Mr Cremlin made Rankin into a completely live human being. It is extraordinary what reality and solidity he can give to a part, provided it is one which fits his personality. Marzo was played quite perfectly. Johnson was very good: Mr Edmund Gurney has a genius for reproducing the stolid self-satisfaction of the working-man.

A FOOTNOTE TO THE ABOVE

March 24, 1906

THE AMOUNT OF time journalists spend in writing about Mr Bernard Shaw is excessive. However, it has to be done; there is no getting away from him. No other writer's work promotes, so naturally, discussion. The public may be near getting tired of the subject; but I believe they still instinctively turn to see what he has been saying last and what can be urged for or against it. They cannot certainly be tired of anything he writes himself.

---

*This reference to Ellen Terry records a fleeting impression of that great actress. Her hesitations were due to the difficulty she was experiencing at this time in remembering her lines. Granville Barker told me afterwards they had to write out passages of her part on pieces of paper which were stuck about the scenery.

In the preface to the novel of his nonage, *The Irrational Knot*, he speaks of the way in which 'the *Carmen* music could enchant a man like me, romantic enough to have come to the end of romance before I began to create in art myself'. Coming to the end of romance is not the same thing as getting rid of it, for it is clear he has not sterilised it out of himself. In spite of philosophical precautions of great antiseptic severity, germs of romance will, occasionally, get into his work and play havoc with it, to the astonishment and exhilaration of beholders. Think of the end of *Captain Brassbound's Conversion*, for example. 'Black Paquito', the rough skipper of a smuggling schooner off the coast of Morocco, and Lady Cecily Waynflete, whose brother, the judge, he purposed to murder for revenge, stand face to face. She has convinced him of the folly of revenge; but in doing so she has robbed him of the aim which lent coherence and dignity to his life. He confesses his helplessness; he is but a rough, staunch, common man, who wants a commander; good under good leadership. Will she—(little did he think, when he served under Gordon, that a woman would be his next captain)—will she be his commander—his wife? Lady Cecily explains to him that such a marriage would appear strange in the eyes of her uncle, the First Lord of the Admiralty, and of her father, Lord Waynflete. 'I care nothing for English society', he cries, and the cry reaches her woman's heart, 'Captain Paquito, I am not in love with you'. Love in the sense in which it is usually understood, she explains, is a *selfish* passion; only through selflessness has she won her power over such men as he. 'Then throw away that last bit of self. Marry me', he replies with irresistible logic and an unconsciously hypnotising glance of his eye. She wavers almost to yielding, when the report of a cannon tells him he must instantly embark. Feeling in his heart, that marriage with him would be a *mesalliance* for her, he kisses passionately her hands, 'I have blundered somehow on the secret of command at last . . . Farewell, Farewell, Farewell'. He goes out with a new purpose and aim in life. What he will aim at as a pirate and a captain of a smuggler, we are not told. All this is certainly romantic.

Now, everybody who has read the play or seen it will be at once struck with the unfairness of this account of a serious scene, which has in reality no little truth and beauty. But is it more unfair than the versions Mr Shaw ordinarily presents in his art of the loves of men and women, with all their confusions and lyricisms and truth; than his presentations of well meaning, windbag Liberals like Broadbent—thanks largely to whom we have for the first time a chance of introducing a taxation upon land values, the first step towards a condition of society which Mr Shaw, as a Socialist, himself approves; or of honest, more or less intellectually and morally self-satisfied and hide-bound men of the Roebuck type, thanks to whom Mr Shaw and all of us can now say what we think with impunity, in print and private—is my account more unfair than these ? *Not a bit!* It is only much less clever.

If he were simply a satirist this would not matter; but Mr Shaw is an artist-philosopher. To the artist we all of us, journalists, critics, reviewers, and public, take off our hats. *The Speaker*[1] has not only made a very respectful sweep before now, but thrown up its wig with delighted admiration. He has created personalities, which people are beginning to use in the short-hand of conversational suggestion as they use characters from Dickens. He has written plays and books that will be read and acted years hence. But he is a philosopher, and he preaches incessantly, with vehemence, theories of right and wrong, about the values of things, and social reform, which are very much open to question. Here comes in the function of the lilliputian army of journalists, critics, and reviewers. We cannot teach him much about his art. But we can probe, twitch, and tug his philosophy to test it, and bring our tintacks and thread to bind him, if possible, to the earth

---

[1] The Liberal weekly for which I wrote and which was destined to turn into *The Nation*.

he 'too untimely scorns', fixing his gaze upon the Superman. Captain Brassbound comparing himself, dejectedly, with Brandyfaced Jack, says that he got his romantic nonsense out of life, while Jack got his 'out of penny numbers and suchlike trash'. It is possible to get unromantic nonsense out of good plays.

THE DOCTOR'S DILEMMA

AT THE COURT THEATRE

November 20, 1906

THIS IS NOT among the best plays. It is a somewhat complicated story, which is made the vehicle of a great deal of hilarious, delightful satire on doctors and of some poor criticism upon the artistic temperament and the place of the artist in society. The story on the face of it looks quite simple: Sir Colenso Ridgeon, the discoverer of an antitoxin remedy for consumption, finds himself with only one vacancy in his sanatorium and two patients. His choice implies a death sentence upon one of them, since the treatment requires his personal supervision—indeed, it is a most dangerous one in other hands. The two sick men are an East End doctor, who is a commonplace honourable man, and a good-for-nothing artist with a real talent. Which life ought he to save? His dilemma is, however, complicated by his having taken a great fancy to the artist's wife. He knows this ought not to influence his decision; nor does it do so directly. But he finds that the wife has no conception that her husband is a worthless fellow; though, it is true, his ways have often landed them both in quandaries which were painful enough. Sooner or later, however, she is bound to find him out—and then what a tragedy for her! This consideration does, apparently, go some way towards deciding the issue in his mind against the artist. I say, apparently, because Ridgeon's motives are not made perfectly clear. This is a defect in the play.

In this dilemma his friend, old Sir Patrick Cullen, is his principal adviser. Sir Patrick is an old-fashioned doctor, a crusty and satisfying character, whose speech is shrewd and kindly, in whom moral work has become at last a kind of intellectual power—a metamorphosis we all have come across in life. When Sir Colenso Ridgeon confesses that his dilemma is complicated by his desire to marry Jennifer Dubedat, in the event of her husband's death, Sir Patrick tells him clearly that he must put that thought out of his mind in deciding; that it is a plain case of good picture or good man. And when Ridgeon, still half hankering after Jennifer, yet half genuinely in doubt, hesitates a preference for good art over good men, Sir Patrick says: 'Don't talk your clever rubbish to me.' Then with solemnity: 'If you live in an age which turns to pictures, plays, and brass bands, because it can find nothing in humanity to ease its poor aching heart, then you may be thankful that you belong to a *noble* and *great* profession, whose business it is to heal men and women.' Once more, after Dubedat is condemned to death, when Ridgeon explains that the principal considera-tion which determined him to cure Blenkinsop was that Jennifer might never suffer disillusionment, Sir Patrick's comment blows to shreds with one puff of caustic sense this phantasmal piece of casuistry: 'It is rather hard on a young man to kill him simply because his wife has too ·high an opinion of him— fortunately many of us are not in that position.' Ridgeon has made the right decision, but on the wrong grounds. Certainly this old Nestor of the profession has the *beau rôle*. Mr William Farren, jun., played him in a way to make one feel, afterwards, that Sir Patrick Cullen must be some one one has known.

The first act takes place in Ridgeon's consulting-room, where five doctors call on him in succession to congratulate him on his knighthood, just conferred. While they are all talking about remedies and discoveries a woman is waiting to see him, and from time to time sends up an urgent request for an interview. Mrs Dubedat refuses to be put off, and at last, through the entreaties of his old housekeeper, he consents to see her. She is told that her husband cannot be taken in as a patient, since the sanatorium is full. But when she shows some of her husband's drawings, their astonishing merit induces

Ridgeon to make every effort to admit him, especially as he likes extremely Jennifer Dubedat herself. He asks her to bring her husband to a dinner at Richmond, where she will meet several eminent men of the profession, and they can all discuss the case together.

In Act II the curtain discovers the five doctors, their host and Mrs Dubedat sitting over coffee and cigarettes: Dubedat has just gone out to put on his coat, preparatory to an early start home. They have all been charmed with the young artist and his wife, except Sir Patrick, who has his suspicions. You cannot tell, he says, what a man is, until you know his behaviour with regard to money and women. Dubedat returns for a few minutes to fetch Jennifer, and they go off with Ridgeon's emphatic promise that he will undertake the cure. Alone together, the five men begin discussing the artist, and it comes out that he has tried to borrow money from three of them, successfully in two cases; and they have hardly got over their dismay, when one of the maids comes in to ask for the address of the gentleman who has just gone away 'with that woman': she turns out to be Dubedat's lawful wife. In addition to these damaging discoveries, poor Blenkinsop enters, terribly upset at having failed to catch Dubedat before he started, because he has borrowed his last half-crown. Before the evening is out he confesses, somewhat reluctantly, to his friends that his own lungs also are touched. Ridgeon decides, after talking over the matter, to save Blenkinsop, and Dubedat is handed over to the mercies of Sir Ralph Bloomfield Bonnington.

Act III Sir Ralph, Sir Patrick, Cutler Walpole, and Ridgeon visit Dubedat's studio to confront him with his misdeeds and to explain to his wife that Sir Ralph will undertake the case instead. Dubedat meets their indignation with dumbfounding placidity. He has no conscience whatever about anything outside his work; but as far as that is concerned he allows nothing to prevent him from doing his best. In this scene he actually tries to borrow money from Ridgeon, on the security of a post-dated cheque, which will enable Ridgeon to blackmail Jennifer into paying him more than he lends.

The last act, in which Dubedat dies in front of the footlights, has been the subject of a good deal of discussion. Mr Granville Barker acted the death naturally and realistically. Fault was found with him on the ground that a death struggle untouched by artistic emotion is an unfair, unilluminating assault on the emotions. But it was necessary that we should realise that chilly, quiet, matter-of-factness of physical extinction, so terribly inconsistent with all we know death means, at the very moment of feeling pity for a man whose will is still ablaze, and whose mind is clear and detached in spite of the creeping languor of death. For Dubedat dies in a pose. He hoards his last strength and his last words to stamp an image of himself on his wife's heart which he knows is not the true one. Next to his immortality in his pictures, he values that reincarnation most. He keeps an interviewer in the room, in the hope that some faint reflection of himself, as he would wish to be remembered, may possibly be thrown also upon the great blank sheet of the public imagination. The cheerful and callous young ass of an interviewer conveys by a few words, after all is over, that he has taken away a grotesquely topsy-turvy idea, such as would have disgusted the dead man and made him laugh sourly enough. That is a telling piece of irony; but profounder still is the irony of the success of Dubedat's pose upon his wife; nothing can henceforth shake her conviction that he is a hero, a king of men. She turns to the doctors, who have let him die because they judged him unworthy, and appeals to them as though they were all standing together on the top of a mountain of transfiguration. In this last scene Dubedat obeyed the same instinct which drove him in life to create beautiful pictures. His last picture is painted on his wife's mind. This is the climax of the play; it is followed by an anticlimax which completes the story.

Ridgeon and Jennifer meet at an exhibition of Dubedat's pictures. She challenges him with being indirectly responsible for her husband's death. 'Confess to a failure and save our friendship.' He admits straight out that he killed Dubedat. But she does not understand at first what he means by this admission. It only gradually dawns on her that he left her husband to die on purpose, and that his motive was a desire to marry her himself, and to shield her from the discovery that her husband was an unmitigated rascal. She is amazed at the idea that he should have been in love with her all the time, and still more at his dreaming she could care for him in return. 'You—an elderly man!' At this reply he staggers back and cries, 'O Dubedat, thou art avenged!' A moment later he hears that, in obedience to her late husband's wish, she has married again, and the play ends with this last exclamation, 'Then I have committed a completely disinterested murder.'

This epilogue is disastrous. Firstly, it tends to trivialise the impression the play has made; for though the last line in it may be, in intention, a summing up of the irony of the story, it rings out fatally in the key of burlesque, like the previous exclamation. Secondly, Ridgeon does not do justice to his own motives; he did not decide against Dubedat entirely because he coveted his wife, or because he wished to save her from disillusionment; so this admission on his part confuses the audience's recollection of what has gone before.

Now to turn to the characters and the acting. Sir Ralph Bloomfield Bonnington (fashionable physician) is a masterpiece. A critic in search of emphasis may choose between saying that the part was worthy of Mr Eric Lewis's acting, or that Mr Eric Lewis's acting was worthy of the part; either statement implies absolute praise. Long will 'B. B.', the frock-coated, rosy-gilled babbler of scientific jargon and impromptu consolations, hang in our imaginations! Mr Lewis's optimistic, confident tenor voice and Micawber-like alacrity of gesture, his air of sympathetic concern, his soothing courtesy of assent as he hovered over his patient or listened to the anxieties of the wife, were perfect. He is at once typical and individual, and, therefore, not simply a caricature. Cutler Walpole (Mr James Hearn) is a caricature of the brusque, hard-headed type of surgeon, whose manner seems to say, 'Pooh, man! the body has no mysteries for us now. Trust me, I'll put that right in a jiffy.' 'B. B.' inspires confidence and holds together a fashionable practice by blandishment and his own natural buoyancy, Cutler Walpole by bluff; both succeed completely in taking in themselves as well. Mr Michael Sherbrooke as the little German Jew doctor, who had scraped together a nice little fortune by using the magic words 'cure guaranteed', was complete, from the gleam of his spectacles to the rasp of his accent. The poor but honest Blenkinsop is almost too worthy an individual to engage real sympathy. After Dubedat has gone off with his last half-crown on the night of the dinner at Richmond, he actually refuses the loan of an Underground fare from Ridgeon, whom he has known for twenty years, for fear his friends should dread his borrowing money on other occasions. This is carrying rugged independence to the extent of becoming a social incubus, and one's sympathies begin to incline towards Dubedat. Mr Gurney found a wonderfully expressive manner for Blenkinsop; a kind of deprecating, big-dog shyness which suggested a loyal, modest nature. Ridgeon was Mr Webster's best part. In appearance he bore an odd resemblance to the Millais portrait of Ruskin. His slightly pompous, educated voice and his self-conscious gestures, both so habitually controlled that they can no longer betray emotion, only express it intentionally, and the suggestions of intellectual refinement in his manner, were all traits of an admirably acted, real character.

Miss McCarthy as Jennifer conveyed the romance of her part. She was admirable when pleading for her husband's life in the first act.

Dubedat was played by Mr Barker as well as the drawing

of the character allowed. He suggested perfectly the character of a rather agreeably uppish, slouching, loose young black-guard at the dinner; and he died well. But the psychology of the character is far too crude to be convincing. The incidents intended to show him up occur with an artificial appositeness, and Dubedat himself is mechanically constructed on the old unsatisfactory formula of 'the artistic temperament', that dismal relic of the art for art's sake movement, so wretchedly barren itself in England.

The avoidance of all artificial appositeness, unreality, or improbability is absolutely essential to the impressiveness of a Shavian play, and the presence of such blemishes is particularly deadly to them for the following reason: Mr Shaw's aim as a dramatist is to correct our conception of the normal, which has been disturbed by a conventional treatment of human nature on the stage. His characters and situations consequently strike the playgoer at first as strange and fantastic; it is with difficulty that he can believe them real; they are so different from what he expected to see. If, therefore, the action and situations deviate in the slightest degree from probability, the whole play, characters and all, in which the ludicrous and astonishing are already so strangely mingled, takes on the air of a fantastic and arbitrary creation. Only the man whose matter-of-factness is above suspicion can convince us that something unexpected is true; and Mr Shaw deals almost entirely with the unexpected. The points at which he has deviated from matter-of-fact plausibility in this play are Dubedat's conduct in the studio and on the night of the dinner; Jennifer's behaviour in the epilogue; and the simultaneous morning visits, of the four doctors with leading practices, on two separate occasions, to the studio of an impoverished artist, where only one had professional business. 'Now', says the spectator to himself, 'the man who will bend facts like this, may well give human nature a twist: I believe this is a clever puppet-show.' He is quite wrong, but the mistake is excusable.

January 3, 1914

IT GOES QUITE splendidly. One is inclined to criticise it in the after-dinner manner of Sir Ralph Bloomfield Bonnington: Delightful evening! Admirable acting! Interesting play! Amusing satire! Charming problem! Stimulating discussion! Hearty applause! Lucky Bernard Shaw! Of course one missed Mr Eric Lewis in the part of 'B. B.' His performance at the Court Theatre in 1906 was one of those rare instances of perfect congruity between an actor and his part which make it impossible to be satisfied with anybody else's impersonation of that character afterwards. Mr Arthur Whitby does very well indeed, but nature has not endowed him with an absurdly optimistic tenor voice or with a natural Micawber-like exuberance. I suggest he should chant passages of his part a little more than he does. I missed the late Mr James Hearn, too, in the part of Cutler Walpole. He was an excellent actor, and though his reputation was not wide, it was a sound and enviable one. Those who saw him play John Gabriel Borkman, when the first shadow of his illness was creeping over him, will not forget the intensity and pathos of his performance. Mr Nigel Playfair, though in some respects the most perfect comedian in London, has not the gift of brusque trenchancy so necessary in playing this caricature of the type of surgeon who, whatever the patient's symptoms, has him down in a jiffy on the operation board and removes something. But in Mr Beveridge, a Sir Patrick Cullen has been found at some points superior to Mr William Farren, who played the part so well when *The Doctor's Dilemma* was first produced. Mr Farren acted the crusty sarcastic side of him better, but Mr Beveridge's Sir Patrick gave an impression of a man of greater *experience*, of a larger nature, one who has learnt the value of rules of thumb in life, and has become, no doubt philistinely, impatient of intellectual subtleties and fine feelings, without, however, losing a jot of sympathy for pain. Like all honest men of common sense, his comments are often as finely penetrating as those of the, so to speak, professionally detached observer. When in Act III Dubedat's imperturbable assurance has floored the doctors who have come to give him a tremendous pi-jaw, and he has gone, they discuss in bewilderment their discomfiture.

> B.B. I shouldn't be at all surprised to learn he's well connected. Whenever I meet dignity and self-possession without any discoverable basis, I diagnose good family.
> RIDGEON. Diagnose artistic genius, B.B. That's what saves his self-respect.
> SIR PATRICK. The world is made like that. The decent fellows are always being lectured and put out of countenance by snobs.

All three are good shots, but the third is really the subtlest comment. For conscience not only (if the proverb is to be believed) makes cowards of us all but fools as well. Part of the price a man must pay for being good is to give up being as clever and formidable as he might be otherwise. Look how the half-cracked and reckless shine in life and in the arts compared with any except the greatest of all! Mr Beveridge's acting while Dubedat was dying and necessarily occupying the centre of the stage was an achievement of which he can be proud. He had nothing to do except sit still and get up twice to attend to the dying man's wants, yet in every gesture, in his look and bearing, he conveyed exactly Sir Patrick's attitude towards the scenic departure. In spite of the absence of the 'only genuine' B. B., I believe this revival of *The Doctor's Dilemma* is an even better production than the one of 1906. Miss McCarthy's acting has gained enormously in sureness and variety of recent years. Jennifer's tenderness and distress were admirably portrayed. She managed in her expression and movements to suggest one who would have been distraught by the agony of watching if she had not had so much to do. Her beauty was blurred in this fourth act as it should have been, till the moment when she returns to the astonished doctors, fantastically dressed in

74

coloured silks, and addresses those indifferent professional men as though the death they have just witnessed together had raised them also to the summit of a mountain of transfiguration. But her dress was not brilliant, beautiful or striking enough. She should have looked like an idol come down from its shrine; rouged and bedizened, glittering and hieratic. The contrast between the impression left on her by the dying Dubedat ("We have shared together a great privilege and a great happiness. I don't think we can ever think of ourselves as ordinary people again") and upon the doctors, two of whom have actually been in conspiracy to let so shiftless a scallywag as Dubedat out of the world as quickly as possible, would then be still further reinforced, and the incongruity between the exaltation produced by sorrow and death and the inevitable ordinariness of life which must be taken up again would have been made still more vivid.

In Dubedat's death scene, Mr Shaw has managed by exhibiting death simultaneously from different points of view, to touch an irony he has seldom reached before. We see death through the indifferent eyes of men who are accustomed to it as a natural phenomenon, through those of a person to whom it is a supremely tragic event, through a facile emotional temperament (B. B.'s), and how it feels to a dying man, artistic and egotistic enough to use it as an opportunity for stamping an impressive image of himself on others. 'Death makes people go on like that. I don't know why it should, but it does', is Walpole's comment on B. B.'s ludicrous outburst of mis-assorted Shakespearean tags. B. B. ought to go on something 'like that', he speaks in his key; but I think it is a mistake to put into his mouth here a speech of mis-quotations which reminds us of the 'Hamlet Soliloquy' in Huck Finn: Dubedat's dying confession of faith, 'I believe in Michael Angelo, Velasquez and Rembrandt, etc.,' has always missed its mark with me and, as far as I can find out, with many other people. It does not ring true, yet it is not meant for a part of Dubedat's pose. If he was the kind of artist we naturally take him to be, 'I believe in Forain, Conder and Gauguin', would have been spoken more out of himself. Certainly from his one-man show as exhibited in the last act no one would guess he cared enormously for Michael Angelo and the rest of them. He had not that sort of temperament. Granted he was a genuine artist, and not the sort of trifler his sketching heads on the back of menus in the second act suggests (a false note that in depicting an artist), he was at best a thorough-going superficial aesthete. Mr Shaw has not put one stroke into drawing his temperament which reveals force of imagination. He has made him too clever, slight and small, to let us believe he was anything but at best a man with a genuine gift for drawing; above all he has made him too clever, one to whom detachment has come too easily to make it likely he was creative. This does not spoil the play, but it makes us rebel when for a moment or two we are asked to take him more seriously. When dying, Dubedat obeyed the same instinct which drove him to paint. His last picture is painted on his wife's mind, not a truthful likeness, but one most flattering to his vanity.

One of the most curious things about the play is that the motive which made Ridgeon resolve to sacrifice Dubedat and save the worthy Blenkinsop instead is never made clear. Did he do so because he thought with Sir Patrick that a good man was more important than a painter of good pictures, or because he wanted to marry Dubedat's wife, or because he wanted to save her from the shock of finding out sooner or later what a poor creature her king of men really was? Probably all three motives actuated him. His last words when he discovers that Jennifer has married again are: 'Then I have committed a purely disinterested murder'. The point of the play, therefore, is not the solution of the problem whether a good man is more worth preserving than a good artist who is a rascal. The play is an absorbing story, with plenty of capital satire on the medical profession thrown in.

THE PHILANDERER

THIS IS A queer piece of work, and finds its place very properly among the 'Unpleasant' plays. It was not very successful at the Court because to make the play intelligible, Charteris must be acted by some one who understands him perfectly, and such an actor probably does not exist. Just as in the playing of Dubedat it is absolutely necessary that the actor should bring out something in his character, to explain why his victims never sent for the police (and this Mr Barker succeeded in doing), so the actor who takes the part of Charteris must make it clear why he is not periodically kicked. He is exasperating and he is disliked, but he was not that sort of person. This can only be conveyed through something in his manner and in his way of saying things. Mr Webster in the part certainly did not appear like a man who gets kicked; but it was his own dignity, not that of Charteris, that was apparent.

Charteris is a very exceptional character. I hazard as an explanation of his immunity and his influence on others, not his wit or cleverness, but the impression he made of being a fantastically honest man; people instinctively felt that he had administered to himself so many moral kickings as to make any they could add an unnecessary impertinence. In one of his talks with the discarded Julia, he says, 'I confess I am either something more or something less than a gentleman; you used to give me the benefit of the doubt.' It is possible, however, to be both at the same time, and that is precisely what he was. Charteris's honesty in his philanderings was morally superior to the code of the conventional gentleman in such matters, which is to continue to simulate respect for the self-respect of the woman, when he knows it to be a sham in which she does not believe herself, in order that she may return the compliment; but on the other hand he fell far below the gentleman in the wanton cruelty with which he used his cleverness to hurt his victims without their being able to understand what he meant. He was not a coxcomb physically or morally, his vanity was superficial; but intellectually he was a cruel coxcomb. For instance, in one of his last interviews with Julia, he exclaims, 'Oh, what I have learnt from you!—from *you* who could learn nothing from me! I made a fool of you, and you brought me wisdom; I broke your heart, and you brought me joy; I made you curse your womanhood, and you revealed my manhood to me. Blessings, for ever and ever, on my Julia's name!' (with genuine emotion, he takes her hand and kisses it). Julia, who does not understand, snatches away her hand, saying, 'Oh, stop talking that nasty sneering stuff.' Where Charteris behaves like a cad, is in not leaving her alone after he has disentangled himself, but in continuing to vivisect her when he knows she can learn nothing from these painful experiments. His general philandering he justified on the ground that it was always instructive to both parties; here he had no such excuse.

Again, the match between Dr Paramore and Julia, which is so much against her natural inclination, is engineered by Charteris to free himself from her persecutions; and there is something so cruel in his using his cleverness and his knowledge of 'the very pulse of the machine' to contrive it, that the spectator is disgusted.

The play, like all artistic work which has aimed primarily at being up-to-date, strikes us now as old-fashioned. It is a product of the early eighteen-nineties, when Ibsen first arrived as a moral prophet on our shores and people went about trying to 'realise themselves;' when the moral of *The Doll's House* was taken as the solution of marriage and sex difficulties; when women were very conscious of being emancipated and determined to sink the 'he and she' in all relations and to 'belong to themselves;' in fact of the period when *The Heavenly Twins* and *The Woman Who Did*, and similar books appeared.

Mr Shaw sympathised with the woman's movement, as his *Quintessence of Ibsenism* remains to show; but as a critical observer he saw clearly enough that many women who went in for emancipating themselves had not thrown off the 'old' woman when they put on the 'new'. This play is a satire which exposes such women effectively enough. However, the 'new woman' no longer exists, nor do such old-fashioned fathers as Cuthbertson and Craven who talk about 'manly men and womanly women;' so the satire directed against them does not seem now to hit a mark worth aiming at.

The kind of comedy extracted from the situations which expose the wretched Julia, is not the kind to make one laugh. A man in the clutches of a jealous termagant might chuckle with delight to see Julia stripped and whipped; but, really, some kind of interested animus is necessary to appreciate this kind of fun; though there are witty things throughout the dialogue which everybody can enjoy, such as this passage for instance.

CHARTERIS. I accuse you of stealing letters of mine.

JULIA [*rising*]. Yes, nice letters!

CHARTERIS.—Of breaking your solemn promises not to do it again; of spending hours—aye, days!—piecing together the contents of my waste-paper basket in your search for more letters. . . .

JULIA. I was justified in reading your letters. Our perfect confidence in one another gave me the right to do it.

Miss Wynne-Matthison played Grace Tranfield, who refuses to marry the Philanderer, with perfect accuracy. The most delightfully-acted character in the piece was Cuthbertson (Mr Luigi Lablache).

DOES SHAW DATE?

January 3, 1925

OF COURSE HE 'dates'. Every dramatist whose methods and criticism of life have impinged immediately and violently upon his contemporaries does so; what seemed most daring no longer startles, what seemed so new appears familiar, and the change is due to him. But when another writer of equal calibre has persuaded the world to look at things from a different angle, the work of the earlier writer, if it has enduring force, will seem once more original. Now the work of Bernard Shaw has this enduring quality. I have been a dramatic critic for many years, and when I review those years, what gives me most satisfaction is that I have always discussed him as a writer of the first importance. Of course I am not alone in this estimate of him; he has many admirers even more enthusiastic than I; but among newspaper critics I plume myself on having consistently and from the first written as though his was a talent we could be certain about. This is a source of gratification to me, for that estimate is not shared by some whose literary judgment I have otherwise good reason to respect. They have never succeeded, however, in shaking my conviction that Bernard Shaw is a classic. I am particularly proud that I have never hedged, because a good superficial case can be made out for his being precisely the kind of writer whom contemporaries overrate: his points are topical, his types date, his themes rise out of social circumstances which dissolve and change. I grant all that. But those who argue thus forget that a dramatist who is not inspired by his own times is seldom inspired by anything. Looking back across a century or two, the mark of 'a classic' appears to be that he was one who was only interested in central human nature, and whose themes were independent of social change or contemporary controversy. We forget that Aristophanes' allusions were as up to date as *Punch* or a 'Max' exhibition, and that *Tartuffe* struck contemporaries as so painfully and immediately applicable that it was suppressed. It is not because a dramatist's themes were topical that posterity, near or far, is indifferent to his work; everything depends on his attitude towards them. The permanent in art can only find vital expression through the artist's interest in the impermanent. What I am proud of as a critic is having always stressed the originality and interest of Mr Shaw's point of view.

Take, for example, *The Philanderer*, running now at the Everyman Theatre, Hampstead, a play which, when published in 1898, was described by the author as a Topical Comedy. Though the salt has evaporated for this generation which knows not Clement Scott, from the speeches of Cuthbertson and his talk about 'manly men and womanly women', and from jokes which in the days when Ibsen and Woman's Emancipation were battle-cries, would have met with crows of delighted recognition, still there remains a genuine exhilarating spirit of comedy running through even those passages of dialogue which have lost sparkle; while beneath all the farce lies a formidable sincerity, immensely and lastingly refreshing. *The Philanderer* is as topical as *John Bull's Other Island*, and 'dates' as much as a revival of that admirable play would 'date' now; but it matters not at all. It 'dates' only superficially.

The Everyman company would no doubt have done better to emphasise its period by dressing the women in the clothes of the 'nineties and following the directions regarding Leonard Charteris's get up. To have done so would have emphasised its internal freshness. The leather sandals were important.

The Philanderer has two themes. One object of the dramatist is to expose the 'womanly woman'; the other is a critical examination of amorous emotions. It may be supposed that the first is now unnecessary. Not at all; the characteristics which are exposed to laughter in Julia have been, and always will be, part of the stock-in-trade of the writer of comedies. The originality of *The Philanderer* lay in the ruthlessness of the exposure. We are tougher-minded than its early audiences, but this only means that the ugliness of the spectacle of seeing Julia flayed inhibits less our enjoyment of the comic aspects of her exposure. It is still an ugly sight, but it is not so shocking as it was, and we are able to notice, what escaped her contemporaries, namely, the withering light which is turned on to the philanderer himself. Charteris is a creation of Mr Shaw's admirable and unflinching honesty; he is a projection of himself in the sense that Tanner is another. When the play was first performed or read, I think I am correct in remembering that William Archer said he felt almost inclined to cut Mr Shaw; the play seemed to him so caddishly unchivalrous. True, there is not a rag left on Julia, but the amatory philanderer, despite his wit, delightful gaiety and even his refreshing freedom from self-deception, is not presented as an admirable figure. He learns from letting himself go in love affairs, and he claims that his victims learn too. He does not shrink from comparing himself with a vivisectionist, but whereas the dogs and monkeys which Paramore sacrifices perish, the young women who emerge from an affair with Charteris have a chance, he claims, of being a little more sensible and honest with themselves and others—in fact with a better sense of human relations and a clearer conception of their own emotions. But Charteris's defence hardly holds good of poor Julia. With regard to Grace Tranfield, a modern audience will be inclined to think Mr Shaw has been a little sentimental. Just as Julia is a first sketch for Ann, so Grace is a preliminary study for the superior women the dramatist afterwards drew. When Charteris tells Julia that from the point of view of morals there is not a word to be said for her, he is saying exactly what Tanner afterwards tells Ann; only Charteris, unlike Tanner, has not yet discovered the point of view from which he can justify his liking for her and keep his own self-respect. The fun about 'Paramore's disease' and the chaff of doctors is as fresh and amusing as ever. The part of Julia requires artistic self-sacrifice on the part of the actress, and Miss Massingham abandoned herself with energetic devotion. Mr Aylmer was admirable as the gentle and stilted goose, Paramore. But neither of the old gentlemen satisfied me, and Mr Claude Rains did not bring out the intellectual passion in Charteris which makes him such a disconcerting, amusing and interesting amorist.

.

THE MAN OF DESTINY

THIS PLAY WAS disappointing. The psychology appeared machine-made and obvious compared with Mr Shaw's maturer work. Bonaparte is compounded and put together here after the Shavian prescription of a great man of action; the ingredients are nervous energy, unscrupulous determination, vanity well under control of the will, histrionic power, above all indifference towards happiness and a reckless disregard for personal dignity and honour, except when something can be gained from them by using them dramatically. The scene is laid in an Italian inn; the time is soon after the battle of Lodi. Some dispatches which Bonaparte expects have been wheedled out of the young blockhead of an aide-de-camp, by a lady disguised as an Austrian officer. The object of this confidence trick on her part was to prevent a private letter revealing some scandal about Josephine reaching the general.

The lady, after getting possession of the budget, puts up accidentally at the inn where Bonaparte is staying. He soon finds out that the young officer described by his lieutenant and the lady are the same person; and the rest of the play is a struggle for the letters. She is willing to hand them all over except one; he will not hear of this. Finally, he bullies her into yielding them all up; after which he reads the letter in question on the sly, and gives it back intact, as though he had been too magnanimous to read it; for he wishes to ignore the scandal, and the only dignified way of doing so is to pretend he knows nothing. When she discovers this, she is overcome with admiration for the courage which dares to do a mean thing, when it suits so perfectly a purpose. The fatuous young lieutenant is under arrest for having lost the dispatches and threatened with expulsion from the army unless he catches the Austrian who deceived him, which Bonaparte knows is impossible. The lady, however, outwits him by dressing up again as an Austrian officer and delivering herself up. At the end General Bonaparte and she are left alone together.

BONAPARTE [*throwing down the letters in a heap on the table*]. Now! *He sits down at the table in a chair he has just placed*].

LADY. Yes; but you know you have *the* letter in your pocket. [*He smiles; takes a letter from his pocket, and tosses it on top of the heap. She holds it up and looks at him saying*] About Cæsar's wife.

BONAPARTE. Cæsar's wife is above suspicion. Burn it.

LADY [*taking up the snuffers and holding the letter to the candle flame with it*]. I wonder would Cæsar's wife be above suspicion if she saw us here together!

BONAPARTE [*echoing her, with his elbows on the table and his cheeks on his hands, looking at the letter*]. I wonder!

Miss Irene Vanbrugh's performance was graceful and spirited. Mr Dion Boucicault as Bonaparte exaggerated his nervous restlessness. He represented him as merely a little demon of energy with fire-flashes of fury and impatience. But it was not only his fault that so little of Napoleon was represented; Mr Shaw himself has not suggested Napoleon's impassable stolidity or his power of investing his *laissez-aller* moods with the air of profound purpose. One feels that Napoleon would have got those letters without making such a to-do about it.

CONCLUSION ON THE
COURT THEATRE

THE ANALYSIS OF these nine plays has not been elaborate enough to require a summary; but there are a few points which may be added in conclusion.

As a dramatist Mr Shaw's gift for caricature is a perpetual temptation to him, leading him often to destroy the atmosphere of reality which is so important to his plays. Though his caricatures are good in themselves, he has not always sufficient artistic self-control to keep them in their places. Moreover, that emotional asceticism, which has been already commented upon, is always tempting him to create in the spectator the balance of mind and emotion he respects by alternately touching him and making him laugh. This method succeeds when the scene, rousing a mixed emotion of sympathy and contempt, is a crude one, such as Broadbent's courting and comforting of Nora Reilly in *John Bull's Other Island*. But frequently this cannot be done by a series of consequent shocks; for the emotion which ought to be roused by Mr Shaw's situations is often too complex and delicate to be produced by such galvanic methods. Sir Ralph's harangue after the death of Dubedat is an instance of its failure.

One character in *The Doctor's Dilemma* remarks, 'Life does not cease to be funny when people die any more than it ceases to be serious when people laugh'. which would be a good motto for most of Mr Shaw's plays. But what he constantly overlooks, as an artist, is that for a man who is feeling its tragedy, life does for the time cease to be comic. He relies, then, as an artist, too much on an exceptional flexibility of emotion in his audience. His weakness as a philosopher is to judge the value of human beings and emotions too exclusively by their usefulness towards furthering another end; as a propagandist, to underrate the intelligence of the average man.

His merits—if my criticisms have not suggested that these are remarkable, I have utterly failed. He has drawn more characters which are immediately recognised and understood than any other English dramatist with the exception of Shakespeare; he has chosen for his subjects situations which are really interesting; and he has made us laugh and think at the same time.

Every author of any power has a peculiar contagion. The contagion that we catch from Mr Shaw's plays is an admiration for courage and intellectual honesty, and for a kind of spontaneity of character which is a blending of both. His plays attack hypocrisy by showing that men have more reason to be ashamed of the disguises of their egotism, than of their egotism itself. The influence of his writings tends to make them found their self-respect rather on their indubitable qualities than on their aspirations, and to prevent them looking for more in life and human nature than they are likely to find. The intention of the greater part of his work is to provide an antidote to romantic despair by forestalling disillusionment, and to stimulate an active and gay resolution in the place of an exasperated seclusion of spirit, or indifference, either gloomy or light. Its danger for some is to breed in them such pride of courage in facing the triviality and ugliness of life, that they come to hate an ideal which may be better than reality, simply because it is not a fact. Mr Shaw often warns us against calling his golden grapes of riches sour, but he has not warned us against disparaging celestial fruits, because they are out of our reach. He has still to write his *Wild Duck*, which I take it will be a satire on 'The Shavians', who derive a perverted gratification from the flatness of life and from the stupendous extent of the social improvements necessary, on account of the scope these offer for the exercise of a light-hearted courage in 'facing facts' and for triumphing over more sensitive natures. All his work is marked by a straightforward dexterity of execution, which is in itself an æsthetic merit; and almost every play he has written stimulates that social consciousness of communal responsibility upon which the hopes of reformers depend.

At the close of such a commentary as this, in which many plays and many actors have been reviewed, it is natural to wonder somewhat anxiously what general impression may have been left behind; to what extent exceptious observations may have seemed to detract unduly from achievement, or how heavily expressions of admiration, owing to a general depreciation in the currency of praise, may have been discounted in the reader's mind. In consequence of such misgivings critics are apt in their conclusions to relax the stringency of their standards, and to fall into a strain of almost obituary benevolence. When the subject of the criticism is some author who has said his best, or some movement which has done its work, such leniency is fitting enough; but here, in the case of this enterprise, which has just finished the first period of its career in triumph, and is starting on the next with public gratitude and enthusiasm behind it, such a tone would be absurdly inappropriate. It requires no coddling at the hands of critics. I have not the least fear that, among those who saw many of these plays, the record of any blemishes will impair the favourable impressions they received; but in the case of those who saw none or only a few, it is necessary to guard against possible misunderstanding, should they ever read these pages.

It is common to complain of the censoriousness of gossip, and to attribute the severity of such comments as pass behind people's backs to ill-nature, when they were really due to the fact that the most *interesting* truths about a particular person happened to be concerned with his faults. In the same way, and for the same reason, the critic finds himself dwelling upon defects; they may even be the defects of good qualities—a needle cannot be sharp at both ends—but if they are more interesting than the merits themselves he is bound to give them close attention. Moreover, from those who give much, much is expected. The reason why criticism is so liable to get out of proportion is that the presence of some real merit is necessary to rouse the critical faculty at all, with the result that such works as possess it do not get praised in the same whole-hearted fashion as those which cannot provoke comparison with high achievement.

The work of the Vedrenne-Barker management has been remarkable enough to challenge the highest standards, and therefore to sharpen the eyes of critics. Certainly (if I may speak for myself) I should not have felt so keenly when anything was lacking in their performances had they not shown me at the same time to what pitch of excellence it is possible to attain.

AFTER THE COURT THEATRE

CAESAR AND CLEOPATRA

April 26, 1913

IT IS NOT likely that Mr Shaw will find again so admirable
an interpreter as Mr Forbes-Robertson for his Caesar;
among the huge farewell audiences at Drury Lane many
must have felt that they had come to bury, not only to praise,
him. Mr Forbes-Robertson's beautiful elocution, his happy
air of intellectual aloofness, his easy dignity, his personal distinction, are properties of incalculable value in a play the purpose
of which is to exhibit greatness of mind, not at the moments
when the hero puts on his crown, but when he is coping good-
humouredly with the pettiness of human nature and the
inconsequent chaos of events.

I have little dramatic criticism, strictly speaking, to offer
this week. What I wish to discuss *a propos* of this most
imaginative play is Mr Shaw's view of great men in general, and
in particular his conception of Caesar. There is, however, this
to be said about the Drury Lane performance: that Act III
could have been better spared than Scene 1. The long speech
of the god Ra was no substitute for Scene 1, which is not only
admirable in itself, but serves to familiarise us, before the
entrance of Caesar, with Mr Shaw's method of handling history.
This method is the same as that which has been used with
infinitely less point by the author of *The Comic History of
England* and Mark Twain, and consists in rubbing off as much
as possible of the *patina* of time from historical characters and
revealing the bright modern colour underneath. Up went the
curtain, and we heard Caesar addressing the Sphinx.

The opening passages of this scene are among the most
admirable in recent drama—Caesar's soliloquy and the small
voice of the frightened girl, who lies between the Sphinx's
paws, answering him. The rhythm of Caesar's speech is not

magical, but how much imagination there is in it, with its fine close: 'I am he of whose genius you are the symbol: part brute, part woman, and part god—nothing of man in me at all. Have I guessed your secret, Sphinx?' And how admirable is the sudden modulation into comedy! Mr Shaw, of course, as a realist philosopher and a child of the comic spirit, must see a hero on the plane of comedy before he will believe in him. To him it is the test of a great man that he should be a hero to his valet, and it is the supreme merit of the play that without the aid of tragedy, poetry, or romance, in the midst of incongruities and laughter, we are made to feel that we are in the presence of a spirit of rare magnanimity and power. But is this man Caesar? Mr Walkley says No: Mr Massingham says Yes, and suggests with intrepidity that Mr Walkley has not read Mommsen; even leaving this an open question, I side with Mr Walkley. I am certain Mr Shaw's Caesar is *not* Caesar. Mr Shaw is a creator; he understands one kind of human greatness so well that he can make us understand it; but any critic can guess where the bias, inevitable in a creator, lies. From among the facts we know about Caesar, a critic could prophesy which of them Mr Shaw would choose as significant, and which he would ignore or flatly disbelieve. Mr Shaw understands the man who leads men, because his will is identified with what he conceives the purpose of the world or of God; who influences them, tames them, though they sometimes end by tearing him in pieces, because he is detached from the passions which possess them; in whom the light of reason, like the clean cold silver of a moon, is never clouded or eclipsed. Absolute disinterestedness, perfect courage—there is Bernard Shaw's explanation of human greatness, and he can create characters which suggest that they possess those qualities. Above all, the test of such a man must be: Is his intellect ever beglamoured or his purpose bent by a sense of his own power or by love of women, whether lustful, or passionate, or poetical? Now in Caesar we might have been sure that he would emphasise his courage, which was indeed an orient virtue in him, his temperance, so marked that Cato said he was the only man who was sober when he had upset the state, his easy generosity, his exact practicality and his splendid, sensible magnanimity; and we might have counted on Mr Shaw unifying these qualities by making them characteristics of an ascetic philosopher who was born looking down from an eminence upon the passions of mankind. Certainly no man resolved quicker or spoke clearer, knowing the edge and weight of every word. But such an explanation leaves much that we know about Caesar incomprehensible.

There is something etherial, something airy, insubstantial, about the man whom Mr Forbes-Robertson impersonates which is hard to reconcile with the idea of the superfine extravagance and dandyism of the patrician youth who first gambled for popularity with a recklessness which broke the rules of his caste, while training himself in all the arts of persuasion and domination, fomenting conspiracies, corrupting justice, distributing largesse, outbidding all his forerunners in display—an epileptic too, who, like Napoleon, found an outlet for an excess of nervous energy in continual excitement and an expenditure of power which would have left other men prostrate. His pallor and queer discordant voice, which he took such pains to control, have been remembered. I cannot see him as possessed of a high impartial aim to rule, but rather as filled with a hunger for *gloria*, glory—to make or destroy something great; flowering at last in a prodigious magnificently all-embracing egotism like Louis XIV's, 'L'etat c'est moi'. It is easier to imagine him demonic than seraphic; the spirit in him not so much the clear light of reason as an infernal god who underground

'With Pluto dwells, where gold and fire is found.'

Remember he was the man who, with all his magnanimity, outraged the Romans by celebrating his triumph over Pompey as though his victory had been against barbarians, instead of over some of the noblest in Rome. If Mr Shaw had lifted from Plutarch that speech of Caesar's to Metellus, who tried to prevent him appropriating the treasury of Saturn—'Thwart me, young man, and I shall kill you; believe me it gives me more pain to say that than it would to do it'—we should have laughed. But the real Caesar was a terrifying man. Mr Shaw's Caesar could terrify the conscience and make people feel miserably small, but I believe Caesar could make the brutal quake, and that he had the manner of one in whom violent passions are only in check.

Mr Shaw would have us believe that Caesar's love affair with Cleopatra was so absurdly trifling that he forgot her existence on leaving Egypt. As a matter of fact, did he not, after that night when the sleek and subtle young queen was smuggled into the palace in a carpet, stay dangerously long? He had come with a half-starved, exhausted army to get fed, and to patch up the quarrel between the Cleopatra and Ptolemy parties, in order to get the tribute owed to Rome by the father of the two rivals. When the Ptolemy party found that the queen had got at him, they knew the game was up. The Roman soldiers were feeding like locusts on the town. Caesar was besieged in the palace, and nearly caught; but after he was rescued did he not, in spite of the urgency of his return (in his absence no officers of state except the Tribunes and Aediles could be elected, and the rabble was out, and ruined men were brooding over the horrors of civil war), in spite of messengers, did he not stay with her two months more?

About a year afterwards he brought her to Rome, and to the scandal of the capital established her and her train in his palace, shocking the pious by setting up her statue in the Temple of Venus, and the Roman citizens by allowing her to call her son Caesarion. Yet Mr Shaw makes Caesar say, when Cleopatra appears as he is stepping into his ship, 'Ah! I knew there was something. How could you let me forget her, Rufio?' As far as I can see, this situation is stark fiction without a rag of probability to cover it. Caesar had a great liking for exotic queens—upon Eunoe, queen of Mauritania, according to Naso, he spent vast sums—and ignoring the more scurrilous gossip of Suetonius, and the distich that his soldiers sung about him at the Gallic triumph, even in the obscurity of a learned language impossible to quote, there is still ample evidence that Caesar was other than the man he is represented to be in the play. He was stupendous, noble, absolutely courageous, a man of great mind, a man of violent passions and personal ambitions, and extremely firm in understanding. He was different; but what does it matter? Mr Shaw has created a great man of another type, not one so likely, perhaps, to have laid down the lines on which the world, being what it was, could be governed for nearly three hundred years, but one well worth contemplating.

CAESAR AGAIN

May 10, 1913

MR SHAW'S ARTICLE in *The New Statesman* on 'Caesar and Cleopatra' has made me neglect my duties. Instead of attending theatres, I have been haunting the Temple of Clio. It is an awe-inspiring place, and on first crossing the threshold a sense of peace envelops one; it seems so sequestered from the fuss and foibles of the world, so august and vast that hurrying footsteps sound impertinent, and voices raised in dogmatic altercation thin and trivial. 'As a tree falls so shall it lie', 'God Himself cannot alter the past'; of such absolute and calming sententiousness are the inscriptions upon its walls. But the irreverent cheerfulness of man is irrepressible, and under the last of these someone had scribbled: 'but historians can'. That this had been allowed to stand seemed to me to argue a vein of ironic humour in the Muse herself, and with spirits somewhat lightened I sent up my credentials, explaining that I was disputing with Bernard Shaw about the character of Julius Caesar, and respectfully begged for an interview. The answer, more considerately worded, was to the effect that the Muse of History herself could not possibly see anyone who had merely pecked about in the past like a sparrow; but that any of her secretaries were at my disposal. This depressed me, for, in spite of the uninviting dangers of the enterprise, I was set upon metagrabolising Mr Shaw, and how could I do this except as an historian? He would not listen to my arguments as a commentator on human nature, for as a theatrical critic I was out of court.

Now, it is perfectly true that if a dramatic critic met (on certain occasions) 'Mahomet or Caesar in the flesh' he might 'put him down as a cold ascetic'; but so might Mr Shaw! Anybody might make that error. The question under discussion is this: if the subject of a play is the love affair between Cleopatra and Caesar, ought not *something* to transpire which would prevent even dramatic critics from making in this case that particular mistake? Mommsen (whom I think Mr Shaw follows too trustingly), even Mommsen, in one of his moments of professorial skittishness, writes: 'the beautiful and clever Cleopatra was not sparing of her charms in general, and least of all towards her judge; Caesar also appeared among all his victories to value most those won over beautiful women.' Now, 'value most' is going a great deal further than I want to go—it seems to me ridiculous; but in a 'Chronicle Play' to put in Caesar's mouth the parting words 'Ah! I knew there was something. How could you let me forget her, Rufio?' seems as wrong in the opposite direction. But, says Mr Shaw, with irrefutable truth, the very first consideration to anyone dealing dramatically with this story of Caesar and Cleopatra must be to distinguish it from that of Antony and Cleopatra. Certainly, even supposing Caesar did stay dangerously long with Cleopatra, he did not, at any rate—

Vit dans ses larges yeux étoilés de points d'or
Toute une mer immense où fuyaient des galères.

And as I write common sense whispers to me: 'Shaw, as usual,
has got hold of the absolutely vital point right enough. You're
a fool to go on hacking and pecking at his work.' But then I
remember the play itself—one of the first, and in some respects
the very best, of modern historical plays; I remember the
homage which is due to the patroness of such plays, the Muse
of History; I remember the entirely pedagogic nature of the
relation between the statesman and the queen as it is represented
in the play, and it seems worth pointing out that, if the case
of Caesar and Cleopatra must be sharply distinguished from
that of Antony and his 'Egypt', it must also be differentiated
from that of Lord Melbourne and Queen Victoria.

In my first article I said that Caesar stayed too long in Egypt
—probably for Cleopatra's sake. Mr Shaw replies that 'Caesar
did not think it too long, and that, as the upshot proved, he was
right.' Now this is a way of saying Caesar and Mr MacCarthy
differ about what Caesar ought to have done 47 B.C.; Caesar
came home, dominated Rome, and proceeded in three years to
lay down the lines on which the world was to be governed
for three centuries—who in this matter do you think likely to
be right? But this is not really fair. The fact is Caesar left
Italy in a state of ruinous misery and confusion to the mercies
of Antony and Dolabella—for an unconscionable time, considering the urgent need for his return. And it must be remembered that in a sense Caesar failed; the hatred and mistrust of his
enemies were too strong for him, and he left his work chaotic,
unfinished. It was the little unlaurelled heads working under
Augustus who made the Roman Empire.

Mr Shaw's conception of Caesar's character forbids him to
admit for a moment that Caesar could have been deflected
from the sanest, most practical course by imagination, passion,
or pleasure. It forces him to postulate that Caesar did not send

afterwards for Cleopatra, but that, like Anne chasing Tanner, she pursued him to Rome. He calls on me to prostrate myself before his picture of a character 'that abhors waste and murder, and is, in the most accurate sense of the word, a kind character.' I do; I knock my forehead three times upon the ground at the feet of the artist; but I cannot believe this man in whom the abhorrence of waste and passion for order were the ruling passions is Julius Caesar. Mr Shaw did not take my point about the effect of transferring Caesar's words to Metellus to the mouth of his own Caesar. I did not object to his Caesar because he was 'squeamish about killing people' (though I think the real Caesar tended, like a Mahomedan, to be magnanimous only to his own people, and that Mr Shaw has made his clemency too philosophical and modern), but to the absence of a terrifying quality in the Caesar of the play which sounds in those words to Metellus, 'Thwart me, young man, and I shall kill you. *Believe me, it gives me more pain to say that than it would to do it.*' I thought this a good point, because in a way that speech is so like Mr Shaw's Caesar, and yet—I felt he had not the fuliginous force in him to carry off its grimness. It seems to suit better the lips of a man in whom the black passion of personal domination was at least as marked as practical reason. And that is the passion which I read in Caesar's career. His ambition coincided to a large extent with the necessities of the world; but the driving force in him was not so much a love of reason and order as the desire of the unscrupulous adventurer for glory in the Roman sense—the desire to make or destroy something great, of one who sat down to gamble at the table of Rome, where *rouge* and *noir* were the democratic and aristocratic parties, staking now on one and now on the other. Mr Bernard Shaw sees in Julius Caesar only certain qualities because he takes a particular view of greatness. He believes that disinterested courage and reason are the real forces before which men and institutions go down. I am sure that is the secret of some great men's influence, but I do not see that the world responds most to these qualities. Great men have been of all shapes and sizes, and the plungers, the colossal egotists, who go so far because they do not know where they are going, seem to me to have drawn even more men irresistibly after them. If that is true, it is a reason for being a republican rather than a Caesarean, in the past, now, and for ever.

ANDROCLES AND THE LION

A RELIGIOUS PANTOMIME

September 6, 1913

ANDROCLES AND THE LION is the most amusing of Mr Shaw's religious plays. He has written two religious dramas, *Major Barbara* and *Blanco Posnet*; one farce, in which conversion is the main theme, *Fanny's First Play*; and then he invented a new form, the religious pantomime, *Androcles and the Lion*. It is the reverse of mediaeval in sentiment and doctrine, but its nearest parallel as a dramatic entertainment is one of those old miracle plays in which buffoonery and religion were mixed pell-mell together. No contemporary playwright, except Bernard Shaw, could write a religious pantomime (Chesterton alone among writers might entertain such an idea), for no other dramatist believes so firmly in the virtue of laughter, is so serious, and delights so much in knocking serious people off their perch. He wants to move you; he cares more about doing that than about anything else; but of all moods, in himself it seems and in others, he distrusts the melting mood most. An English audience has not as a rule sufficient emotional mobility to follow a method which alternates laughter with pathos, philosophy with fun, in such rapid succession. Consequently his plays generally divide an audience into three sections: those who take in only the funny bits (they are the majority, so his plays are popular), those who attend chiefly to the religion and philosophy (some of whom dislike them or are bored), and those who are irritated and puzzled by the two elements being so thoroughly mixed together. Among the last are to be found most of his critics. But no one can have appreciated a religious play by Bernard Shaw *as a work of art* who has not, if tears come naturally to him, cried, and then laughed so soon afterwards that he has forgotten that he cried at all.

However often one may have criticised Mr Shaw, and I have done so many times, it is exciting to do it again. One always feels as though one was going to discover something new to say about him after seeing his last play; the walk back from the theatre on such occasions for a critic with a taste for his profession is a fine pleasure. What I am going now to say may not be new, but it was borne in on me with fresh force after seeing *Androcles*. Most of the critics of the play have spoken about his indiscriminate satire, his mockery of martyrs, his raising a cheap laugh by treating disrespectfully what is usually treated with reverence. In the more indignant of these criticisms there was something of that vulgarity and obtuseness which led the last Lord Chamberlain to ban *Blanco Posnet* as a blasphemous play. *Blanco Posnet* seemed blasphemous to the Censor because a horse-stealer, burning with the fires of conversion, did not express his feelings with conventional reverence. It is easy to understand a man, if he hates religion, feeling repelled by anyone in Posnet's state of mind, whether the zealot happens to be General Gordon, Wesley, or a horse-stealer. I can understand his disliking martyrs next worst to the people who make them. It is possible to hate religious zeal and be an exceptionally admirable man like Bradlaugh, Voltaire or Samuel Butler. But to allow good taste and convention to get between you and the recognition of the very thing you profess to and do reverence elsewhere, and then to call it blasphemous or mean is vulgar and inhuman. I am no theologian, but as far as I was ever able to make out what was meant by that mysterious sin against the Holy Ghost, so severely penalised that it really might have been more clearly defined, it was a deep, wilful, damnable unfairness to which this kind of obtuseness is certainly akin. My discovery about Mr Shaw was that his most striking merits as a writer spring from his being marvellously free from that obtuseness and all forms of spiritual snobbery. I do not mean that he sees everywhere what is most important, far from it; in some directions he seems to me quite blind, but whatever he does admire in human nature that he will see wherever it may be, and honour equally. Often he discovers it in situations and people where it is so buried in incongruities, or so smarmed over with bad manners and bad sentiments, that his recognition of it suggests to people that he is satirising the thing itself. In the case of this play many have apparently thought that because the meek little martyr, Androcles, is made to talk namby-pambily, and the gross, chaotic Ferrovius to parade his inward wrestlings and bawl the phrases of a hot-gospeller, the dramatist was satirising the religion of these men. That is obviously a mistake—their tone, their sillinesses, yes, but not their faithfulness.

Ferrovius is explained with sympathetic insight. Lavinia says (it shocks him dreadfully for the moment) she would like to see him 'fight his way to heaven'—that is to say, to obey his instinct and use his temper, his masterfulness, and his sword. While into the mouth of the henpecked, inconspicuous Androcles is put one of those lines which summarise a character and delight a critic. He is too humbly pacific to fight for his life in the arena, too incapable of resentment, so he asks, rather with the air of a tired man timidly excusing himself for taking a seat in a full waggonette, that he may be allowed 'to be the one to go to the lions with the ladies'.

There are four types of religious zealots represented, all of them fundamental enough to have existed in the second century just as they exist now. Androcles is the 'pure fool', the sort of little man who nowadays might go about in fibre shoes and an indiarubber coat to avoid using the skins of animals and drink almond milk with his tea. Yet in him burns a little flame of courage that no wind of misery or torment can make flicker. The drawing of his character is an instance of Mr Shaw's recognition of the qualities he admires in whatever character they may happen to be found. Ferrovious belongs to the type of 'born again', overwhelmingly manly, internally miserable, fighting parson, who sometimes gets into a scandalous mess to the horror of his flock, the amusement of the world, and his own scorching remorse. His religious life, apart from taking others by the scruff of the neck and compelling them to come in, is a continual struggle to acquire the Christian virtues of benevolence and submission and an inner freedom and peace. Born a servant of Mars and ignorant of himself, he has become a follower of Jesus of Nazareth. He, too, reveals himself in a sentence; he is terrified to think that he may betray his Master when he finds himself in the arena and give stroke for stroke. 'When I feel a sword in my hand I could as soon throw it away as the woman I love from my arms. Oh, what have I said? My God, what have I said?' He recovers confidence in himself by officiously exhorting the others to pray as they are hustled into the arena; but face to face with the gladiators the sudden glory of battle seizes him and he stretches out all six of them, to return again over-whelmed with remorse and shame. The delighted Emperor pardons all the Christians to commemorate such a feat of arms. He declares extravagantly that he will insist upon every man in the Pretorian guard becoming a Christian, and offers Ferrovious a place in it. Ferrovius, remembering perhaps Lavinia's words about fighting his way to heaven, accepts. His prayers and wrestling for the grace of Christian meekness have not been heard, and in the arena he has come to understand his own nature. 'The Christian God is not yet', he mournfully concludes. 'I strive for the coming of the God who is not yet', is Lavinia's response to that.

Lavinia is the third type of martyr. She is the kind who goes to the stake with *nearly* the smallest possible amount of definite belief that she is, so to speak, in the secret of the universe. An after-life, a martyr's crown, mean little to her; purgatory and hell nothing at all. She is only certain of this, that the whole point of being alive and all satisfying happiness lie in obeying an instinct to identify herself with the will of the world which is thought of as divine, and that instinct prevents her from submitting, even by an act of formal recognition like dropping a pinch of incense on an altar, to a cult which stands in the way of her religion. The dialogue between her and the Captain of the Guard is one of the best serious passages in the play; it is quite short, but there is a great deal in it. He is rather in love with her, and he uses all the arguments that have been used against martyrdom to persuade her to sacrifice to Diana. He appeals to her scepticism, to her good taste as a lady and Roman (why make a pompous, hysterical fuss about a mere form), to her common-sense and self-respect (you're simply committing suicide and not even doing anything fine). To that last argument she has a reply which makes one think with that momentary intensity which often leaves a mark on one's permanent opinions: 'Death is harder for us Christians than for you.' She means *she* has something which she really wants to live for.

The fourth type of zealot is Spintho, who does not know what faith is. He is lashed on by his own misery and terror and lured by the hope of currying favour with superior powers. In a particular case he turned tail and was accidentally eaten by a lion; but he is the sort of creature who swells the ranks of every persecuted cause or religion and makes it all the harder for genuine people to fight or suffer for it. He usually attracts the almost undivided attention of persecutors who want to justify their conduct. As the centurion says while he is cuffing and shaking him, 'You're the sort as makes duty a pleasure.' Mr Shaw has omitted two other types of martyr: the man who goes to the stake with something very like a bad conscience (he is rare, but he is interesting and, I think, lovable), and the martyr who sacrifices himself because he simply thinks certain definite dogmas are true. Mr Shaw holds that such men do not face death for their creed. If this play were an historical drama this last omission would be a serious defect, but it is not, and I have, while discussing the thought in it, almost forgotten that

it is a pantomime. Other critics, however, have described the
fun, the inimitable lion, the Emperor, the call-boy of the
Colosseum, who announces the next item on the programme
in the familiar voice: 'No. 11. Lions and Christian women.' It
was the thought and feeling in this delightful entertainment
that needed further comment. Coming out from the theatre,
I heard one man say to another: 'But what's the point to the
whole thing?' 'Oh', said his friend, 'it's a skit on plays like
The Sign of the Cross and *Quo Vadis*. That's what it comes to.'
I was jammed up close against them and I could not help
saying: 'I think it would be nearer the mark to say that *The
Sign of the Cross* is a skit upon it.'

PYGMALION

April 18, 1914

PYGMALION? IT LOOKED like a misnomer. The story of Mr Shaw's play on the face of it was that of an artist who turns a live girl into a work of art, and then by a considerable effort of self-control refrains from falling in love with her! It is an exhilarating, amusing, and often a deep comedy, and it is admirably interpreted at His Majesty's. Like all good comedies, it is full of criticism of life; in this case criticism of social barriers and distinctions, of the disinterested yet ferocious egotism of artists, of genteel standards, of the disadvantages of respectability, of the contrast between man's sense of values and woman's, and of the complexity and misunderstanding which a difference of sex introduces into human relations, however passionately one of the two may resolve to sink the He and She. During the course of the story, light—and sometimes it is a penetrating ray indeed—is thrown into all these corners of life. I hardly know how to tackle a play which bristles with so many points, especially as I must confess that I am not certain I understood the play as a whole. Has it an idea or does it simply bristle? The merriment of intellectual antics is in it; the wit of penetration: 'the difference between a flower girl and a duchess is not how she behaves but how she is treated'—there is a good deal in that comment upon manners. Mr Doolittle (so admirably played by Mr Gurney) is Mr Shaw's most amusing achievement, in his Dickens vein of exaggeration. Doolittle (if he were a horse he might be described as by High-Spirits out of Social Science) is the philosophy of 'the undeserving poor', incarnate and articulate. He does not exist; but he is sufficiently like a type to make one fancy Nature may have been aiming at him. All the minor characters are well drawn.

PYGMALION

Henry Higgins is an extremely interesting study; Eliza
is excellent, but she is interesting chiefly from her situation
—a flower-girl who after six months' training at the hands
of Higgins, the professor of phonetics, can be passed off
in society as a lady. That, of course, is the story, the simple
circumference of the play; but where does the centre of
interest lie? In the relation between Pygmalion-Higgins
and Eliza-Galatea? I thought so while I was in the theatre,
and my feelings at the end of the play were in one sense
highly flattering to the dramatist, to his power of entertaining and interesting, for when the curtain fell on the mutual
explanations of this pair I was in a fever to see it rise on
Acts VI and VII; I wanted to see those two living together;
I wanted to get to the *point* which I conceived was still ahead.
Afterwards I grasped what I now take to be the idea: there was
point in the title *Pygmalion* after all; the statue did become alive;
Acts II, III, and IV, during which Eliza was being moulded
into a lady, were not the miracle, but merely the chipping of the
statue itself from the rough block; but in Act V something
happened, she had got a soul, and therefore the play was really
over. I felt inclined, however, to credit myself with uncommon
penetration when I discovered what had happened to Eliza
in the fifth act. Perhaps when I read my fellow critics I shall
discover that what I found with effort was quite obvious to
them. In that case I retract in advance the criticism that Mr
Shaw has huddled up his climax, and failed to arrange the
perspective of the dialogue so that the mind is led easily up to
the central point. Now the last act is, and is not, a love scene;
Pygmalion-Higgins, like other Shavian heroes, is running away
from passion, and Sir Herbert Tree acted admirably his nervous-
ness, his dread of even touching Eliza lest the floods of irrational
emotion should be released in himself. The experiment is over;
it has been a triumph for his art as professor of phonetics; Eliza
has passed through the stage of talking like a flower girl with a
mechanical meticulous pronunciation (Act III); she has become,

109

both in the matter as well as the manner of her conversation, indistinguishable from a born lady; Higgins has won his wager. She has run away from him because she has found intolerable his tyranny and his disregard for her as a human being with feelings (Act IV). All along she has shown a spaniel-like docility and gratitude which he has never thought of recognising. He has fagged her about right and left; she has become useful, almost necessary to him in practical ways; but the more she tries to please and touch him the more harshly impersonal he becomes. But when she runs away he is frantic to get her back. The question is on what terms; he won't offer her anything more than he gave her before and does not understand at first that she only wants to be treated like a human being. Then she turns on him: threatens to his dismay, to go off to his rival with all the secrets of his art; in short, shakes him off and stands on her own feet as an independent human being. The statue has become alive, during the six months' hard training she had acquired the outward signs of self-respect, but she never had the inward reality till this moment. Henceforward she is a person he can reckon upon, and his fear of her disappears. That I take it is the theme of the play.

Higgins is called a professor of phonetics, but he is really an artist—that is the interesting thing about him, and his character is a study of the creative temperament. We have met him before in an early novel by Mr Shaw; he is Mr Jack the composer in *Love Among the Artists*. The gesture with which Higgins flings money at Eliza in the first act after browbeating her, the chivalry and roughness of it, is a repetition of the scene at Paddington when Jack gives all the money he has in his pockets to Gwendolen to whom, by the bye, he also subsequently taught elocution, bullying her into perfection and bitterly disappointing and puzzling her by treating their relation, which had begun so romantically, as a sternly matter-of-fact impersonal one the moment she became his pupil. Jack thought only of the job in hand. If, on the one hand, he treated her as though she were a machine he had to get into order, on the other, when he had made her a fine actress he no more expected gratitude from her than he did from the paper on which he had written a sonata. Higgins behaves in the same way to Eliza. Like Jack he has a total disregard of people's feelings, he is outrageously inconsiderate, and yet he is most human. His impatience is the impatience of the artist who only asks Heaven for peace to devote himself to his work. Sir Herbert Tree's acting was delightful at all points where the comedy rests on the comedy of anyone so incapable of self-control as Higgins teaching deportment; he did not, I thought, bring out forcibly enough the violent sincerity of the character. The professor has that absolute self-dependence, that attractive combination of egotism and disinterestedness of artists with creative force in them.

Act IV is the most dramatic of the five. The three of them have been out to a fashionable dinner; Eliza has been perfect. She is to all intents and purposes a *lady*. The two men begin talking, Eliza sits apart. They are triumphant and tired. What a grind it has been—oof! it's over *at last*, what a blessing, what a triumph! While they are talking like this in her presence, there she sits, stony, miserable, stunned (how good Mrs Patrick Campbell was!); Higgins has not the smallest inkling of what all this drilling and training has cost Eliza herself, or how hard she has tried to learn. It has been hard enough work for him chipping the statue out of the block, but the marble itself has suffered more.

PLAY V. FILM

July 1, 1939

THOSE WHO SAW *Pygmalion* in 1914, when Mrs Patrick Campbell played Eliza Doolittle and Tree the part of Higgins, will notice where its colours have faded and where they have kept as fresh as ever, while a comparison of this revival at the Haymarket with the extremely successful film of the play points to a fundamental difference between screen and stage.

The part of Eliza was written for Mrs Campbell. There are passages in it which could only have been written by a dramatist who delighted in the temperament of that great actress as well as in her art; and was set on using, not only her unrivalled grace and elocution, but a strain of Italian peasant in her: she would make, he saw, a perfect flower-girl as well as a perfect lady, while remaining most potently herself. I have been told—or perhaps I read it in Mrs Campbell's own Memoirs?—that when Mr Shaw first read the play aloud, she cried out at one point, "You wretch! that's *me*." No other actress could have smoothed so perfectly Eliza's manners, or have flung Higgins' slippers in his face with such spirit. Inevitably, those who remember Mrs Campbell's acting will find Miss Wendy Hiller's somewhat tame, though to say that is hardly adverse criticism. No doubt colour has faded from what was the brightest dab of it in her part; the moment when from the lips of an apparently refined Eliza the word "bloody" fell among the tea-cups of a Chelsea drawing-room—a word till then unheard in any theatre. But today, the English Rose is capable of coarser expressions than that; and Eliza's comments on her aunt's death, which once only led up to the climax, now actually strike the audience as more amusingly incongruous with her appearance and deportment. True, "bloody" still gets its laugh, but it no longer releases the roar that greets the crash of a taboo.

On the other hand the theme of Pygmalion is as fresh as it was; namely, that class-distinctions are uncivilised; that the worst manners spring from class-consciousness, and class-consciousness from differences in pronunciation and accent. The self-absorption of Higgins's makes his behaviour as inconsiderate as lack of education makes Eliza's, but at least he treats everyone alike. He may be rude, but his rudeness is not discriminating.

Mr Shaw has always championed Equality and Fraternity,

though he has never been sound on Liberty, as the recent development of his views has revealed. Because neither Nature nor Society allows complete freedom to the individual, he seems to think that the contribution that comparative freedom can make to human happiness is unimportant. His reasoning on Liberty seems on a par with that of those who argue that because our press is not free from capitalist control, there is nothing to choose between it and the dictated press of Totalitarian States (I have just come across that argument in Chesterton's *The Resurrection of Rome*), or with the contention that since popular representation is most imperfect, it might as well be scrapped. Today, the worst enemies of the people are those who shout that Democracy is not democratic enough for them. They are often cryptic Fascists; Mr Shaw is not one, but he plays their game. However, *Pygmalion* is an old play of his, and in the lamentations of Mr Doolittle (spouted with great spirit by Mr George Merritt) on finding that £3,000 a year does not compensate him for the loss of the disreputable freedom he once enjoyed, I detect at least some recognition of a connection between liberty and happiness.

The difference between the general effect of the play and the film is striking, considering that much more care has been taken to absorb the dialogue intact than is usual in play films. Mr Shaw, I expect, insisted that his points should not be left out, or his theme ignored. And yet the general effect of the film *Pygmalion* (and that accounts for its immense popularity) is merely that of a wish fulfilment love story of a poor girl who became a lady and married the man who made her one. I hazard the explanation that this enormous difference is due to a peculiarity inherent in the art of the cinema itself. On the screen we are much more affected by what we see than by what we hear. This would account also for screen-dramas being more restful entertainments than plays. Dialogue which stimulates thought is inevitably swamped by Impressions conveyed pictorially. How seldom we remember anything that was *said* in the cinema!

MR SHAW ON CHRISTIANITY

June 3, 1916

EASY READING OFTEN makes hard reviewing, as I am now finding to my cost. Mr Shaw's new volume includes *Androcles and the Lion*, *Overruled*, and *Pygmalion*, and a long preface on Christianity and its founder. I shall take for granted that the plays are familiar and discuss only the preface. This in some respects is the worst piece of work he has done; it shows all his faults, all his limitations. As is the case with every writer, there are dumb notes in his piano; but in this piece Mr Shaw sits down and strums on them. On the other hand, there are passages in it which are as permanently valuable as anything he has written. His subject is religion. Those who know his works will anticipate where, on this subject, he will write like a seer and where he will show an invincible ignorance. They will be sure beforehand that the tone will be jocular, jaunty and positive, as though the writer could not conceive any sensible person differing from him, and as if reverence were an emotion which is at best a duffer's virtue, and more usually a dishonest form of sentimentalism. They will be sure, too, of meeting in the book a rare spontaneous sincerity, which, as long as its power is upon them, will enable them to pursue their own thoughts with more vigour and directness. Compared with Mr Shaw other contemporary preachers seem smitten with the-fear-of-giving-themselves-away disease. Although often wrong, he is more irreplaceable than anyone. I do not know what we should do without him.

Those who believe Jesus is God will find this preface intolerably blasphemous. To those who do not believe that, but to whom Christ is, nevertheless, a sacred personality, in some way vaguely conceived as infinitely and unapproachably good, it will seem intolerably flippant; and its tone may seem offensive even to those who are vastly more sure that, being a man, he was imperfect, than that they can censure him rightly. For although Mr Shaw's whole contention is that Jesus of Nazareth was one of the greatest of men, he does not make the reader feel the nobility and beauty of his spirit. He seems afraid of doing that for fear of not making him a real person. 'You may', he says, 'deny the divinity of Jesus; you may doubt whether he ever existed; you may reject Christianity for Judaism, Mohammedanism, Shintoism, or Fire Worship, and the iconolaters, placidly contemptuous, will only classify you as a freethinker or a heathen. But if you venture to wonder how Christ would have looked if he had shaved and had his hair cut, or what size in shoes he took, or whether he swore when he stood on a nail in the carpenter's shop, or could not button his robe when he was in a hurry, or whether he laughed over the repartees by which he baffled the priests when they tried to trap him into sedition and blasphemy, or even if you tell any part of his story in the vivid terms of modern slang, you will produce extraordinary dismay and horror among the icono-laters. You will have made the picture come out of its frame, the statue descend from its pedestal, the story become real, with all the incalculable consequences that may flow from this terrifying miracle. It is at such moments that you realise that the iconolaters have never for a moment conceived Christ as a real person who meant what he said, as a fact, and as a force like electricity, only needing the invention of suitable political machinery to be applied to the affairs of mankind with revolu-tionary effect.' This is absolutely true; I respect Mr Shaw more than ever for having written it. But unfortunately when Mr Shaw makes the picture come out of the frame the figure is not in the least like Christ; it is indeed the most preposterous travesty, with all the beauty and nearly everything that mankind has loved and that *is* in the Gospels, left out.

Here is Bernard Shaw's portrait of Christ. Though, like John, he became an itinerant preacher, he departed widely from John's manner of life. John went into the wilderness, not into the synagogues; and his baptismal font was the river Jordan. John was an ascetic, clothed in skins and living on locusts and wild honey, practising a savage austerity. He courted martyrdom, and met it at the hands of Herod. Jesus saw no merit either in asceticism or martyrdom. In contrast to John he was essentially a highly-civilised, cultivated person. According to Luke he pointed out the contrast himself, chaffing the Jews for complaining that John must be possessed by the devil because he was a teetotaller and vegetarian, whilst, because Jesus was neither one nor the other, they reviled him as a gluttonous man and a winebibber, the friend of the officials and their mistresses. He told straitlaced disciples that they would have trouble enough from other people without making any for themselves, and that they should avoid martyrdom and enjoy themselves whilst they had the chance. 'When they persecute you in this city',he says, 'flee into the next.' He preaches in the synagogues and in the open-air indifferently, just as they come. He repeatedly says, 'I desire mercy and not sacrifice', meaning evidently to clear himself of the inveterate superstition that suffering is gratifying to God. 'Be not, as the Pharisees, of a sad countenance', he says. He is convivial, feasting with Roman officials and sinners. He is careless of his person, and is remonstrated with for not washing his hands before sitting down to table. The followers of John the Baptist, who fast, and who expect to find the Christians greater ascetics than themselves, are disappointed at finding that Jesus and his twelve friends do not fast; and Jesus tells them that they should rejoice in him instead of being melancholy. He is jocular, and tells them they will all have as much fasting as they want soon enough, whether they like it or not. He is not afraid of disease, and dines with a leper. A woman apparently to protect him against infection, pours a costly unguent on his head, and is rebuked because what it cost might have been given to the poor. He pooh-poohs that low-spirited view, and says, as he said when he was reproached for not fasting, that the poor are always there to be helped, but that he is not there to be anointed always, implying that you should never lose a chance of being happy when there is so much misery in the world. He breaks the Sabbath; is impatient of conventionality when it is uncomfortable or obstructive; and outrages the feelings of the Jews by breaches of it. He is apt to accuse people who feel that way of hypocrisy. Like the late Samuel Butler, he regards disease as a department of sin, and on curing a lame man, says 'Thy sins are forgiven' instead of 'Arise and walk', subsequently maintaining, when the Scribes reproach him for assuming power to forgive sin as well as to cure disease, that the two come to the same thing. He has no modest affectations, and claims to be greater than Solomon or Jonah. When reproached, as Bunyan was, for resorting to the art of fiction when teaching in parables, he justifies himself on the ground that art is the only way in which the people can be taught. He is, in short, what we should call an artist and a Bohemian in his manner of life.

No array of terms can express my contempt for this portrait. Mr Shaw, in painting it, has neither as artist nor as philosopher tried to get out of himself. He has not paid his subject the respect which would have been due even had his subject been one of the meanest of mankind instead of one of the greatest— namely, of treating him as someone different from himself. There is an egotistical delusion latent in this picture: all great men are *really* like me. And in the same way Mr Shaw's historical sense is controlled by the same delusion; all times (with the exception of a few beliefs in demons or divine incarnations) were really like my times. The corollary he draws is: 'To revive the real Christ I have only to attribute to him my religious sense, and to imagine him as living not 2,000 years ago in the East, but now, and in England.' This is utterly false. The result is as unreal as anything achieved by Archdeacon Farrar.

You know the way self-assertive people take you up and say quickly, 'Yes, yes, you mean to say this', and then proceed to utter their own opinions. Mr Shaw has treated the doctrines of Christ in that way. He gives a fallacious account of them; he has ignored what he does not agree with as not what Christ meant. The whole essay is a compact discourse on a theme announced in the first section: 'After contemplating the world and human nature for nearly sixty years, I see no way out of the world's misery but the way which would have been found by Christ's will if he had undertaken the work of a modern practical statesman.' According to Mr Shaw Christ's teaching may be summed up as follows:

(1) The kingdom of God is within you. [This Mr Shaw does not fully understand, though in one respect no man who writes understands it better.]

(2) Get rid of property by throwing it into the common stock. Dissociate your work entirely from money payments. You cannot serve both God and Mammon.

(3) Get rid of judges and punishment and revenge. Love your neighbour as yourself, he being, literally, part of yourself. And love your enemies: they are your neighbours.

(4) Get rid of family entanglements. Every woman is your mother; every man your brother.

The second contention is that these precepts can only take effect through political reforms; that Christ taught the true religion, the religion of communistic socialism.

Now, all these four precepts are in the Gospels. They are an important part of Christ's doctrine. But Mr Shaw's interpretation of Christianity is fundamentally wrong, because it is the interpretation of a man who is a prophet of a State conception of life. Whereas Christianity is a religion which regards the life of the individual soul and its relation to God as the end, declaring therefore states of the soul to be ends in themselves, and the contemplation and love of God to be supreme ends, towards which freedom from the world and personal ties are means to those ends, religion, as Mr Shaw feels it, is a mystical impulse tending towards social progress. His religion is a religion of the social conscience. He preaches a God whom it is impossible to adore, for He is ourselves. Our life is not to adore or feel but only obey, and in obedience is to be found the only happiness worth having. He misunderstands Christianity because he interprets Christ's doctrine as merely a reiteration of the prophet's injunctions not to think religion lies in sacrifices and ceremonials, but in being just and kind, which implies, of course, an entire reformation of society. Thus he misses the inwardness of Christ's morality. The famous 'blessings' in the Fifth Chapter of Matthew are almost all concerned with a man's inner feelings, not with his outward actions, with what he *is* and not with what he does. Mr Shaw understands by 'The kingdom of God is within you' only an inward allegiance to duty. And he writes as though no other kind of religious emotions existed. One can go further than that and say that there is in all he writes an implicit contempt for contemplation.[1] He believes he is preaching the religion of the future, or rather the only one that can save mankind. I do not believe that. The doctrine that all men are members one of another may be assented to in a sense by everyone some day, and men may act upon it. But that they will necessarily love each other does not follow; it may still be a loveless world. One is inexhaustibly kind and indulgent to oneself; one can admire oneself; but love oneself—that is impossible. How, then, can you teach men to love each other by proving or asserting they *are* each other? The weakness of Christianity seems to me to lie in asserting that love is within the power of the will. But where it is vastly superior to Mr Shaw's religion is that it keeps alive, and puts before everything those moments when men see each other as worthy of all the love they can feel.

---

[1] In *Back to Methuselah* he afterwards attempted, but failed, to present the contemplative life.

DARK LADY OF THE SONNETS

MR SHAW ON SHAKESPEARE

June 20, 1914

HISTORY HAS UNFORTUNATELY hung the portrait of Shakespeare in a bad light. Like some dark, rich, glazed master piece in an ill-planned gallery, it seems to reflect not infrequently something of the features of those who peer curiously into it. Shakespeare has often been compared (an ill comparison) with Nature herself. If the comparison holds at all, he was most like Nature in this: that it seems only too easy to read into him whatever you have a mind to read. Sir Sidney Lee's Shakespeare is essentially a steady man, one who, farming judiciously an inexplicable talent, gathered much comforting gear about him during life and died honoured, safe, satiated, and prosperous; Sir Leslie Stephen's a stoic who was no pipe for Fortune's fingers to play upon. Mr Frank Harris's Shakespeare, on the other hand, is a man as intellectual, book-minded, and will-less as Coleridge himself, as tremulously sensitive too, who, to the perpetual advantage of mankind, was pitched, shivering and longing, into the roaring rapids of the world, there to struggle vainly in the whirlpool of his own passions and appetites, there to be pounded and twisted and tossed and washed at last, a poor broken empty shell of himself, into a little bay rocked gently by the drumming thunder of the falls. Mr Harris's Shakespeare has a treble dose of sensuality in him; he is a sweet-natured sort of man with a hunger for all pleasant, bright things, for happiness and the amenities, and no heart at all to condemn any man for anything except downright cruelty. Never did gentler spirit 'affront the long humiliation of life'. He showed flashes of ferocity and anger when excruciated, but his anger had no sort of root in

pride to nourish it, and was most placable. He could forgive
Life as easily as men when they smiled on him, and as easily
fall to cursing her again. He had 'two loves of comfort and
despair', but no philosophy; fate played its plain fugues and
pæans on him as on an instrument. He was the friend of
picturesque scallawags and adored gaudy noblemen. He
talked, laughed, drank, swaggered, worked, loved—above all,
loved—wept, suffered, and wore himself out. Such, in its
essentials, is the picture of Shakespeare in Mr Harris's wonderful psychological study: 'no hero I confess', but such a one to
whom mankind nevertheless holds out its arms and greets with
Cleopatra's greeting:

> O infinite virtue! Com'st thou smiling from
> The world's great snare uncaught?

Uncaught? That is the point to discuss. Uncaught in a sense,
but mauled and broken, having been torn by the teeth of many
snares.

Then Mr Shaw comes along and says: 'Frànk, you're a
wonderful fellow. There's no one to touch you at all as a
Shakespearean interpreter. But you've no sense of humour;
at least, it's in abeyance, swamped by your great capacity for
scorn and pity. You don't understand the main fact about
genius. Genius is gay; it's gay. Pity in you demands that
Shakespeare should be a broken man, whose sweetness exhales
from having been brayed in a mortar. Nonsense: genius is the
faculty of rising superior to life. The characteristic of a dramatist
of genius is that he can "discover comedy in his own mis-
fortunes almost in proportion to the pathos with which the
ordinary man announces their tragedy. . . . I cannot for the
life of me see a broken heart in Shakespeare's latest works."
Why, Frank, you're not going to tell me a big pot like that was
set boiling by a flame for any dark lady. Have not I proved to
the world that a man of genius is a man essentially immune

from the weakness and trivialities of the passions?' And as we read we see the shadowy portrait of Shakespeare taking on an air of familiar and indomitable detachment. Mr Frank Harris's sympathy, according to Mr Shaw, is misplaced. It is the dark lady, or ladies, he ought to pity.

The man who 'dotes yet doubts, suspects yet strongly loves', is tolerable even by a spoilt and tyrannical mistress; but what woman could possibly endure a man who dotes without doubting; who knows, and who is hugely amused at the absurdity of his infatuation for a woman of whose mortal imperfections not one escapes him; a man always exchanging grins with Yorick's skull and inviting 'my lady' to laugh at the sepulchral humour of the fact that, though she paint an inch thick (which the Dark Lady may have done), to Yorick's favour she must come at last?

It is a case of Jupiter and Semele over again; 'it was not cruelty that made Jupiter reduce Semele to ashes; it was the fact that he could not help being a god nor she help being a mortal.' You see, Mr Shaw, in a subtler sense, remains after all among the bardolators: Shakespeare was superhuman. Years ago he wrote one of the finest pieces of modern criticism proving that, compared with Bunyan, Shakespeare had no sense of the heroic life or turn for drawing a hero; yet when it comes to summing up his character, he will have it that he was, after all, made of that stern stuff. He could not have been at the mercy of life. Mr Shaw points out that if any man could look the ugly facts of life in the face with a chuckle, it was Shakespeare; certainly a Shakespeare without irony and gaiety would not be Shakespeare. In such lines as Richard III's:

> And this word 'love' which greybeards call divine,
> Be resident in men like one another
> And not in me; I am myself alone—

he sees his fundamental attitude towards that passion. Of course Shakespeare could often 'be hugely amused at the absurdity of his infatuation', whether for a woman, fame, riches or for life itself; but he must have been also quite as often contemptuous or oblivious of that amusement; otherwise he could never have written the poetry which makes men feel that he has said their best for them. I have not read Mr Harris's play. I dare say Mr Shaw's criticism that the poet appears as a depressing victim, a pitiable broken man with a grievance, is true. But I have read Mr Shaw's play, *The Dark Lady of the Sonnets*, and anything less like a poet than the principal figure in it, I can hardly imagine. Of course, the qualities Shakespeare shows there are consistent with being a great poet, fun, promptness, airy courage, and a relish for fine phrases, but they do not make a great poet. Mr Shaw leaves out the belief the poet must have that his own feelings are wonderful and that the objects of his desires and admiration are supremely worthy of his art. The fact is Mr Shaw will have it that a great man must be in a deep sense invulnerable. He thinks of genius as a kind of immunity from average human weakness, bringing with it an irrepressible gaiety of heart. This is the chief difference between him and Mr Harris. To me it is easier to imagine Shakespeare as Mr Harris describes him, as a man even more at the mercy of all that tortures and beglamours than average mortals, with an enormous overplus of sensibility which even *his* intellect and vital resilience could not control. His towerings of gaiety and lyrical happiness seem easier to reconcile with such a temperament than his power of expressing extremest pain, pleasure and longing with the idea of a man planted beyond the range of their direst power. In some poets—Dante, Milton, Wordsworth—one feels a fundamental mastery and detachment, but not in Shakespeare. Who would invoke him at a crisis: 'Shakespeare thou should'st be living at this hour'? We feel instinctively that if he were he would probably be far too occupied in living to detach himself and help.

AUGUSTUS DOES HIS BIT

SYNGE AND SHAW

January 27, 1917

A DISCOURSE OF SOME profundity might be written upon the Stage Society's programme last Monday, but do not hastily turn the page, I shall not attempt it. Both *The Tinker's Wedding* and *Augustus Does his Bit*, both Synge and Mr Shaw, the juxtaposition of their work, and its reception by an English audience, suggest reflections upon the nature of comedy and the uncommonness of appreciation of it, which might lead one very far from those plays themselves; both of them are characteristic, but by no means prime examples of their authors' talents. All I shall try to do is to jot down a few reflections, in order to suggest to the reader, if he has a turn for criticism, the better article he might have written himself.

When pictures are hung for exhibition, the chief problem is to arrange them so that those hung side by side should not kill or disparage each other; some pains are usually taken that the spectator should be spared (he is expected not to be very nimble in appreciation) the gymnastic feat of looking for quite different qualities in the very next picture that arrests his attention, or at any rate that the qualities it lacks should not be precisely those which he has just enjoyed. Perhaps it does not matter as much as the hanging committee thinks; but it does matter, it matters just as much in the case of other kinds of art.

Synge's comedy is the comedy of naturalism; Mr Shaw's is the comedy of exaggeration. In Synge's comedy there is both pain and beauty; Shaw's is intellectual and extraordinarily good-natured and has no beauty. Now, one of my impressions the other night was that *Augustus* suffered by proximity to *The Tinker's Wedding;* all the more so because the audience did not respond to the gaiety of the latter. They could not digest it. They listened, so it struck me (I am sensitive to the impressions of my neighbours), with the solemnity with which they would have listened to *The Tragedy of Nan*. To them *The Tinker's Wedding* was a study in rural depravity (a drunken old woman in a ditch) inexplicably blended with the tomfoolery of putting a priest's head in a sack. They perceived the dialogue was beautiful, which made them feel more solemn still. It is not true that an Englishman takes all his pleasure sadly, but he is very apt to take his aesthetic pleasures with an awful gravity. Queen Eleanor, presenting fair Rosamund with the alternative of the dagger or the poison cup, is the image under which I think of the expression on the face of the British public when receiving a work at the hands of a poet. Such was the mood in which *The Playboy of the Western World* was first received by them here. Laugh? Dear me no, I thought they would have died. The play might possibly have "knocked 'em in the Old Kent Road", had it been performed there, because in that locality they are not without a sense of the sardonic; life teaches it to them. But the West-end finds it more difficult to appreciate the humour which has pain for a neighbour. It has a kind heart (as far as the imagination is concerned), the West-end, but it is not robust. If Dickens had not made it a rule to be sentimental on every other page and had not been obviously exaggerative, a good many of his studies in human nature would have been thought no laughing matter. However, now that *The Playboy* has been performed so many times in London, and people have been told that Synge was a great man and knew what he was about, they do laugh. They know it is all right now; though if they saw that play performed with due savagery (they never have) perhaps they would have doubts again.

The Tinker's Wedding disappointed, too, in another way. It is not full of funny lines; the comedy lies in the whole—in the conception. The audience was not prepared for this. Where were the jokes? True, there was one speech which amused. When that old reprobate Mary Byrne wakes up in the ditch and sees Sarah washing for her wedding, she says: "That's fine things you have on you, Sarah Casey; and it's a great stir you're making this day, washing your face. I'm that used to the hammer, I wouldn't hear it at all; but washing is a rare thing; and you're after waking me up, and I have a great sleep in the sun.' Any remark about washing, or rather not washing, is, of course, safe to get its laugh in an English theatre. A hip bath, not the cross, ought to be the symbol of our religion. But that you can have a fine comedy without a single funny line in it (funny at least to those who have not grasped the comic conception underlying the whole) is a truth few believe in. In short, the verdict of the audience upon *The Tinker's Wedding* seemed to be that of Queen Victoria on a famous occasion, 'We are not amused', and they settled down to be really amused by Mr Shaw. He certainly did not starve them in the matter of funny lines; but an odd thing happened. Although they had not grasped the comic conception underlying Synge's play, in a dim way they must have felt it was there, because the amusing digs and exaggerations, the jokes good and bad, the thistles for donkeys and neat exposures of incongruities, of which *Augustus Does His Bit* is composed, sounded trivial, the crackling of thorns under a pot. I surmise this partly from the quality of the laughter evoked at the time, and partly from the very sniffy comments of my most respect-worthy colleagues upon that skit the next morning. They must have missed the absence of the comic idea in Mr Shaw's fantasia, and resented the far-fetchedness of its connection with actual fact. Following a play in which the comedy lay in reality, and required an emotional detachment, we were asked to appreciate an extravaganza which required detachment from common sense, and had only a distant relation to fact. Synge did not amuse because his subject seemed serious, and no jokes were perceptible; Mr Shaw did not really amuse because only jokes were perceptible, and he did not seem serious enough. In fact, the plays did not help to show each other off. Only people of exceptional nimbleness and detachment could shift in each case to the mood in which to enjoy either of them. I hasten to add that it is only in retrospect I find it easy to do so.

The best jokes in *Augustus* were jokes at the expense of administrative regulations which have an unforeseen backwash. To take for a change an example from the country of our enemies of the kind of thing against which these jokes were mostly directed. The other day in Germany a municipality, looking around for something new to tax suddenly remembered cats. No doubt they carefully estimated the number of these pets. The results were disappointing: only seventy-two cats survived, while the mice and rats increased at such a pace that the tax had to be removed and urgent orders given that it was the patriotic duty of every citizen to breed as many cats as possible. At the end of his conversation with his 'staff' at Little Pifflington, one old drunken, stammering man (Mr Rock was admirable), all Lord Augustus can do is to boom 'Go! or I'll charge you under the Defence of the Realm Act with discouraging me.' The height of extravagance which the farce reached may be gauged by the fact that Lord Augustus at one point produces from his pocket a bullet which has been flattened by contact with his skull. After that it is a little hard to criticise Mr Shaw for not making his 'silly soldier man' a real person. The piece ought to have been acted with wild spirits, which were noticeably absent from Mr Sharp's performance; and it ought to have been taken in the spirit of a revue by his critics. People won't take Mr Shaw lightly enough when he is doing the Dan Leno stunt, nor seriously enough when he is serious. I am not saying it is not partly his own fault, for he claims that he is always serious, and he cannot resist a joke whatever he writes.

It was a great pleasure to see Mr W. G. Fay again. The unobtrusive perfection of his tinker was all that might have been expected from him. Miss Maire O'Neill was so good as Mary Byrne that it would debase the currency of praise to bestow it on anyone else after mentioning her name.

THE SHOWING UP OF
BLANCO POSNET

February 24, 1917

VISIONARY DRAMA IS not suitable for chamber performance.
On the other hand, in the case of realistic plays, like *The
Showing Up of Blanco Posnet*, to be forced by pro-
pinquity into feeling as though one were oneself on the stage is,
once the imagination has consented to believe in the characters,
a positive advantage. I always dislike a distant seat in a theatre,
not because I cannot see and hear well enough, but because the
bodily presence of the actors works on me much more powerfully when I am near them. Mr Fisher White's acting as
Blanco Posnet was admirable, and doubtless it impinged on
me with greater force because I could see the vein swell on his
neck when he roared out his favourite adjective 'rotten', and
observe the desperate fixity of his glazed and choleric little eye.

When the curtain went up, discovering a number of small,
clean women in sun-bonnets, shucking nuts round a table in a
barn, I said to myself, knowing what a tearing, flaring, revivalist
drama was ahead: 'This will never do. Do they think they are
going to dance an old country dance?' But the moment the
action began and Blanco came on the scene, I felt the performance was going to be all right. And it was.

The things the women were saying were interesting. Mr
Shaw is a first-rate hand at supplying minor characters at once
with a point of view. They were discussing horse-stealing and
lynching. Their remarks sketched for us the moral of this
pioneer outpost of civilisation, where a trial in the Sheriff's
Court is only an appetiser to stringing up an unfortunate
wretch and having shots at his twitching body. It is a community
where every man feels it treason to his manhood to show mercy

or admit to fellow-feeling; where it is 'turning soft' to act upon such emotions, and 'being a sniveller' to appeal to them in others. This fundamental principle of their morals must be kept in mind, or the spiritual contortions of Blanco Posnet, his desperate anxiety 'to keep the devil in him', to die game—that is to say, full of hatred and contempt—will be half-incomprehensible.

When he is dragged into the barn to await his trial for horse-stealing he is in a strange, excited state. This state of mind is admirably depicted. A feeling of freedom, power and reckless-ness possesses him, but this feeling, which impels him to provoke in others precisely that bullying blackguardism he now despises with a new-born relish, is shot with self-contempt and with amazement. Joy and misery, a craving to dominate and smash, a craving to abase himself and utterly forget himself in others, fight within him and tug him to and fro. The spectacle (presented to us with extraordinary psychological sympathy) is that of a certain kind of man in the throes of a religious conversion. The illumination, or whatever you like to call it, has taken place only a few hours before. He is still in a devastated, heaving condition. The centre of gravity of his emotional life has not yet shifted permanently; he does not yet know if the sense of a universal life which he lately felt flooding him and glowing in him is mirage, or if the unwholesome, obscene, personal passions which spit at him from the mouth of Feemy Evans and gloat at him out of the eyes of the jury represent realities among which a man must live, giving what he gets. 'A plague on both your houses' is a cry that would express his soul. When he is introduced he is trying to recover a foothold upon his old conception of life, but it quakes beneath him. The curses of Feemy, the humbug sanctimony of his brother, and the oafish, homicidal humour of the Sheriff, anxious not to keep the jury waiting for their sport, bring with them a sense of home, of certainty, of satisfaction that he will soon be quit of this 'rotten' world of 'rotten' blackguards. He is desperately afraid of being left alone, and the company of his canting brother, Elder Daniels, is a relief to him. When Daniels begins to try to bring him to 'a proper state of mind' before death, and also in the same breath to find out what has become of the horse, the moment he mentions God Blanco breaks out:

> He's a sly one, He's a mean one! He lies low for you. He plays
> cat and mouse with you. He lets you run loose until you think
> you're shut of Him; and then, when you least expect it, He's
> got you.
> ELDER DANIELS. Speak more respectful, Blanco—more reverent.
> BLANCO [*springing up and cursing him*]. Reverent! Who taught
> you your reverent cant? Not your Bible. He says He cometh
> like a thief in the night—aye, like a thief—a horse thief.

It was this passage which shocked the censor. What had happened to Blanco Posnet was this. He had spent the night with his brother, Elder Daniels, in this little town, and as a sort of make-weight for legacy money he failed to get out of him, he went off in the early morning with a horse out of the stable. The horse was not Daniels', but had been borrowed by him off the Sheriff. When Blanco had ridden some way he met a woman carrying a child choking with the croup to the doctor. She asked for help. After cursing her and the child he gave her the horse, knowing that his life went with it. This action was instantly followed by an experience such as has often been recorded in religious biography. He went off waving his arms and singing. Then he sat down staring at a rainbow, which seemed to have a message for him written on it; sat stunned with joy and bewilderment till his pursuers came up and quietly took him. His inward excitement was so great that on looking back he hardly knows now if the mother and child were visions or realities.

While the trial is proceeding towards the foregone conclusion, and he is fighting all he can (suggesting that Feemy,

who saw him on the horse, is too unclean to kiss the book, etc.)
there is a noise on the door. Someone rushes in to say the
horse is found; a woman stole it, and she is there too. At this
news Blanco becomes violently agitated. Her child is dead;
when she comes in, the sight of her grief-stricken face silences
the Court. Blanco shouts: 'She ain't real. That's the woman
who brought me to this.' He begins raving about the choking
child, and when she denies that Blanco was the man who handed
her over the horse ('The man looked a bad man. He cursed
me, he cursed the child',), the Sheriff suggests that as the lady
may have a delicacy in swearing away a man's life, Feemy had
better do the job. Feemy shows the greatest alacrity, but when
it comes to the point of saying the words they stick in her
throat. So the end of the trial is that the Sheriff declares it is
not a case of horse-stealing to commandeer a horse to save a
child's life, and Blanco jumps on the table and delivers a
harangue, the substance of which is that everybody's rotten
and a fraud, that bad men only pretend and swagger as bad,
that there is nothing but a 'rotten game' and 'a great game', and
that when he played the great game he lost the 'rotten feeling'
though he cursed himself for a fool. In fact, he makes the sort
of speech one often hears at street-corners, only it is not a
repetition of what once was spontaneous, but an utterance
wrung out of him by torture and by joy, and therefore moving.

There are two flaws which prevent this play being a permanent
source of satisfaction. The first occurs when Feemy breaks
down: 'Oh, God! he felt the little child's hands on his neck—
I can't'! she exclaims, and she bursts into tears and begins
abusing the mother. This strikes one as theatrical and sentimental. She may have felt what the words express; the tears
are all right, but one is not convinced that this is the way she
would have expressed her feelings. Even 'I can't' alone would
have been more effective; and the abuse of the mother, 'You
with your snivelling face', is just an overdose of sentimental
theatricality, a rubbing it in which Mr Shaw should have been

above. He has put himself into this little drama, but he has not forgotten himself in it completely. Blanco, when he delivers his address on salvation, asks the question, Why did God allow 'the innocent kid to die', and save him? 'What about the croup? It was early days when He made the croup, I guess. . . . When it turned out wrong on his hands, He made you and me to fight the croup for Him.' This piece of philosophy is false to character. It is an importation from the mind of Mr Shaw himself.

The play is a moving and strongly sentimental tract. It might interest and exhilarate thousands 'who find the only God adapted to their worship in every tie of natural affection and every thought of natural respect that binds them to their fellow-men.' But, thanks to the Lord Chamberlain, it can only be performed in holes and corners. What sort of unfermented dough must serve for brains those whom he relies on I cannot imagine.

BACK TO METHUSELAH

July 9, 1921

THERE IS ONE generalisation about Mr Shaw's works as they have appeared volume by volume which I have never seen made, though I have read many books and articles about them, namely, that there are a great many more ideas in his prefaces than ever get into his plays. This is only natural, but often the ideas which are most emphasised in those prefaces and make them impressive find only a subordinate or an indistinct expression in the dramas when the curtain goes up. This is not true of his early prefaces and plays, but it is true of most of the volumes he has published since *John Bull's Other Island*. The early prefaces were really aids to critics; but how few, for example, of the important ideas on education and family life ever got out of the preface into *Misalliance* and *Fanny's First Play*, or how little of that indictment of people's states of mind, and feeling during the war, which will make the preface to *Heartbreak House* live, was ultimately reflected in the dialogue or action of that play! This generalisation will not seem unimportant the moment its implication is grasped: that for the last fifteen years, with some exceptions, Mr Shaw has not written the plays which express directly his most important ideas on the subjects he dramatised. Of course, the plays have been the offspring of his ideas and have been influenced by them, but they have not (with a few exceptions like Pygmalion) been the embodiment of them. This time he is sure he has written in *Back to Methuselah* the play he ought to have written. Yet he is mistaken.

He has written an impressive preface insisting on the paramount importance of religion for the individual and for the race, but he has produced five plays, in which there is hardly a

134

gleam of religious emotion, and in which the religion he believes in himself is never shown as inspiring or influencing anyone. True, Adam and Eve and Cain in the Garden of Eden talk a little about the Voice and what it says to them; but the essential thing about these figures is not their communion with anything without or within them, but that they are represented each as bundles of specialised instincts and aptitudes into which the Life Force has divided itself in order to achieve its ends. *Blanco Posnet* and *Androcles* are religious plays, so is *Major Barbara*. In them you see religion acting upon men and women. In these five plays we are given a series of glimpses of the course which, according to Mr Shaw, human progress ought to follow and of the goal it can attain, if men can be persuaded to believe in Creative Evolution. Some of the reasons for believing in it are given in the preface. You must believe first that the reason why a giraffe has a long neck is that for many generations certain beasts with short necks have willed to have long ones. Well, if you are not familiar with the idea of natural selection, which also fairly plausibly covers the phenomenon, that may not be hard. The point is, that once you have believed that the will is creative, you can then be happy about the future of mankind, because they can will themselves in the long run into a state of eternal perfection. Of course, willing is not a matter of taking up a Geruda stone like Mr Bultitude and wishing you were a boy again; it is a state of perpetual effort, conscious and unconscious.

Now, there is a drawback to the universal acceptance by mankind of Mr Shaw's religion which has nothing to do with the evidence for or against it. It is this. It only meets the needs of a particular and rather rare type of man. Mr Shaw, no doubt, would deny this, but he can only do so from a mystical point of view, not from the evidence afforded by the way men behave. He would say, "We are members one of another; all religions assert it, and even science, by giving us a common ancestry, admits it. In that case the deepest and strongest passion in all of us must be a devotion to the whole race. What each of us cares most for is the fate of mankind. Therefore, the religion which would really satisfy us is one which would enable us to foresee the endless progress of mankind towards perfection." It is true that we are concerned, when we are reminded of it, and some of us profoundly, about the future of the race. It is a detestable thought, when it is vividly put before us, that the cosmic process may wipe out mankind altogether. The most eloquent passage in Mr Balfour's *Foundations of Belief*, which is really a pamphlet of intimidation—believe or you will be unhappy—calls up the picture of a dead world. But so is the idea of our own death detestable, when we really envisage dying. Yet we manage partly by forgetting, and partly by staring death out of countenance now and then when we are feeling calm and powerful, to accommodate ourselves to the idea; and it is far easier to become reconciled to the death of the race some millions of years hence, of which we are not so often or so vividly reminded. In short the instinct which makes us take to heart the welfare of mankind is only one of many, and it is the only one which the religion of Creative Evolution satisfies.

In Mr Shaw himself it is the predominant one; even his instincts as an artist are subordinated to it. He has said again and again that he would not have written a line if he had not wanted to make men better and more sensible. (His impulse merely to amuse and excite them and make them admire is stronger than he thinks it is, but that is another matter, and he explains himself to himself in that respect by saying that 'every jest is an earnest in the womb of time', which is a doubtful generalisation.) In the last play in this book art is put in its proper place as the creation of dolls for children, since it can no longer illuminate the path of progress. The point is, that Mr Shaw is a born reformer and therefore he cannot see that the religion of Creative Evolution has any defects.

A born reformer must be an optimist; this religion affords

a basis for optimism: 'We fail, we die, it does not matter; the ends we strive for will be attained at last by those who come after us. The individual is of no account.' Mr Shaw's religion gives him that assurance and he needs it urgently because, when he looks round him, he does not by any means take an optimistic view of mankind's chances of improvement. When he wrote *Man and Superman* he took refuge from disillusionment in the idea of eugenics. We are under the feet of the swinish multitude; even the educated are ignorant and petty idiots for the most part; we must breed ourselves into being a better race. In the preface to *Back to Methuselah* he confesses that 'the circumstances of this catastrophe (the 1914 war), the boyish cinema-fed romanticism which made it possible to impose it on the people as a crusade, and especially the ignorance and errors of the victors of Western Europe when its violent phase had passed and the time for reconstruction arrived, confirmed a doubt which had grown steadily in my mind during my forty years' public work as a Socialist—namely, whether the human animal, as he exists at present, is capable of solving the social problems raised by his own aggregation, or, as he calls it, his civilisation.' In fact, he wants another injection of optimism to be able to go on with any heart. It has crossed his mind that life is short (he is not far off the end of his own), too short perhaps for any man to master facts and learn wisdom. As the whole of creation (remember the giraffe's neck) shows that where there's a will there's a way, let men, therefore, will to live for three hundred years, and afterwards for a longer period.

The idea looks silly, but I have been a close reader of Mr Shaw for many years, and often his ideas which first struck me as silliest were the ones which I subsequently found had modified my thoughts most. There is no reason why science should not discover how to prolong life. I do not believe it can be done in the way in which Mr Shaw seems to believe, and the late Mrs Eddy believed it could be done, but if men determine to find out more about the nature of growth and decay and of their own bodies, they may make the necessary discovery. In that case, a world full of vigorous men and women of much greater experience than we can ever have would certainly stand more chance of progressing rapidly towards a better civilisation. It is an idea worth storing in the armoury of hope.

Perhaps the most stimulating psychological idea which emerges from these plays is the suggestion that it is the consciousness of the shortness of life which makes men so scatterbrained and ready to snatch at all sorts of things which do not belong to their peace. So little else seems worth while. Longevity would steady them; it would then be worth while to look forward. In the last play, 30,000 years hence, the 'ancients' have ceased to care about anything that men now usually pursue. All the desires and experiences which make up the value of life for us are compressed into the first three or four years of existence, a brief childhood, starting from the stage which we regard as that of completed manhood. Just as in the womb now the child goes through all the stages of physical development which preceded man, so emotionally and intellectually the whole of experience as we know it, is telescoped into the first few years of human life after the new being has emerged perfectly grown from the human egg. They afterwards become 'ancients', immortal and *sans* everything, except the passion for contemplation and one practical preoccupation (Mr Shaw being a reformer cannot envisage a static state of bliss)—namely, how to get rid of the body altogether, and reach—what?—Nirvana. God or Life will at last, through the agency of man's brain, disentangle itself from matter completely. That is the goal of the cosmic process according to Mr Shaw.

What he has attempted to write is not a series of plays with religion for its theme as an agent working in the minds of men, but a kind of Hegelian cosmology in pictures, which plausibly approximates to what conceivably might happen, if it turns out to be true that a giraffe has a long neck because its forebears have willed to have one, or if a carrot is red for the same reason.

In the first play, he uses the myth of the Garden of Eden to indicate the relation of man to the cosmic process; in the second he gives us a snapshot caricature of the sort of men in whose hands the future of mankind resides; in the third the coming of the longer-lived men; in the fourth he contrasts the short-lived, ignominious, childish creatures we are with the tremendously superior beings who have each had hundreds of years' experience, and the last play takes us to the edge of the Absolute itself. It is an extraordinarily imaginative effort, but not an artistic success; the proportions are wrong. Some profound things are said by the way and not a few absurd ones.

BACK TO MR SHAW

October 11, 1924

WHEN *BACK TO METHUSELAH* was brought to London an accident prevented me from seeing it, but the newspapers all those weeks kept assuring me that I was not missing much. The long and short of the reports which reached me came to this: that *Methuselah* was 'rather' wonderful but distinctly boring. I went last week to the Court Theatre to see Part V, 'As Far as Thought Can Reach'; I listened with riveted attention. Once only did I feel impatience—when Pygmalion was explaining how he had made his two live dolls, an impatience which the dramatist had tactfully made the audience on the stage also share. *Methuselah* is a tremendous effort of the imagination on the part of a man who in some directions has obviously deep insight, to express his sense of the meaning of life. It cannot be boring to anyone who even in the interstices of wool-gathering, work and distractions, has tried to think—unless such a person has thought beyond the dramatist. To the commoner class of person, the vague sceptic and amateur of philosophers (among whom I include myself), such a work must be interesting, if the ideas in it are passionately presented; and that is certainly the case here. The vague sceptic is not likely to be convinced by *Back to Methuselah*. If he has the habit of making a pillow of his doubts, he is a very difficult person to convince; not another philosopher, but some irrelevant incident in his own life is more likely to twitch that pillow from under his head.

It is not hard to classify Mr Shaw as a philosopher. He is an evolutionary pantheist, with pronounced Manichean sympathies. If he had been an Early Father he would have opposed the doctrine of the resurrection of the body tooth and nail. The aim of his 'ancients' is to get rid of the body and all the values which derive from it; they long to become mere 'vortices', whatever that may mean, in the Universal Spirit. Naturally, the furthest stage towards this ideal at which they can be dramatically presented is that of the Buddhist saint. And the impression made by these clean, cool, bald, gentle old creatures, with mysterious psychic powers (admirably acted by Miss Edith Evans and Mr Cedric Hardwicke) is, on the stage, exactly that of Buddhist saints, far advanced in disentangling themselves from the wheel of life, but still far from Nirvana. Christianity is too personal and 'human-all-too-human' for Mr Shaw; even the Indian doctrine of Karma (the doctrine of retribution imaginatively extended) is apparently repugnant to him. In the place of reincarnations, in which the individual in the course of ages works out his salvation, sometimes missing a stage if he has been very good, sometimes beginning again lower down if he has been bad, he has imagined the life of each individual as, barring accidents, indefinitely prolonged. To those who are inclined to look upon religions and philosophies as expressions rather of what the heart in each case needs to believe, rather than of what reason and observation have suggested, the religion of *Back to Methuselah* is the one we might have expected Mr Shaw to hold. He is a born reformer and his religion is comfortable, and therefore credible, only to those of the same temperament. 'This is the true joy in life', he wrote years ago, 'the being used for a purpose recognised by yourself as a mighty one; the being thoroughly worn out before you are thrown on the scrapheap; the being a force of Nature instead of a feverish, selfish little clod of ailments and grievances complaining that the world will not devote itself to making you happy.' The passage (Preface to *Man and Superman*) was one of the most spirited and permanent he has written; and that preface will always be a trumpet call to the reforming instincts in men. All his religion is implicit in it. What the born-reformer needs from religions is faith in a Cause —nothing else matters so much. It must be a Cause ultimately triumphant, and it is even more inspiring to him, if he can also conceive it, as an unending progress, since the idea of finality is distasteful, and even synonymous with languor and death, to such temperaments. When Mr Shaw wrote *Man and Superman* he was already growing sceptical about particular political and social reforms. Man must be born again and born different, or it was useless to tinker society; eugenics was the hen-coop to which he clung in the wreck of earlier hopes. After the war he propped up his forward-looking optimism with another postulate. Life was too short for even the well-born to learn wisdom: men must will to live for centuries—for ever. For the young are too occupied in satisfying other instincts to centre their minds upon making the world better. So in *Back to Methuselah* he conceives as inevitable a state of human society in which four years after birth everyone reaches the physical detachment of old age, and all the glamour which sex, animal spirits, the delight of the senses lend to experience then vanishes. Intellectual curiosity remains for them, and then since this would be indeed too bleak a world, the adult are conceived as enjoying also a kind of religious ecstasy, which Mr Shaw has been too active a man himself to express, as an artist, in the masterly manner he has suggested other human emotions. Moreover, he has finally placed his faith out of reach of discouragement. If the human race fails to reach spiritual perfection, the Life Force will scrap it and begin progress with another kind of being (see Lilith's closing speech). Thus even the idea of the most terrible calamity which a reformer can envisage, the failure and extinction of the race (he can support with courage his own failure), cannot henceforward touch Mr Shaw's optimism. This is an example of what is called 'the will to believe'. The propositions to which this faith commits a man are, it is hardly necessary to say, doubtful, and when believed they are only satisfying to a portion, and a small portion, of mankind.

The chief defect of the production was that the picture of life as enjoyed by the young was not sufficiently attractive. The most effective part of the play lies in criticism, from the point of view of religious asceticism, of aesthetic and amatory emotions. The case of their vanity has been yet more strongly put, but it is well put here. The superb merit of the play is that it is the work of an artist who has asked himself, with far greater seriousness and courage than all but a few, what is the least he must believe and hope for if he is to feel life is worth living.

HEARTBREAK HOUSE

October 29, 1921

H EARTBREAK HOUSE IS one of the most interesting
of Mr Shaw's plays, just as it is undoubtedly the queerest
and subtlest of them, and perhaps (so far as the phrasing
of the dialogue is concerned) even his best-written play. It
has, however, defects which might confuse any audience, and,
what is worse, it contains incongruities glaring enough to
offer some excuse even for contempt, from such as are either
too unobservant, too unemotional or too prejudiced against
Mr Shaw himself, to perceive the acute profundity of his
criticism of modern society or the noble desperation which
inspired the play.

Mr Shaw's indifference to Art, or that side of it which deals
with methods and form, has recoiled on his own head before,
but never with such annihilating effect. He will merge the
artist in the prophet, and the result is that as a prophet he does
not get the hearing he deserves. Look at the Press criticisms
of this play! They have been disgraceful, but it is not to be
wondered at. Probably every night there are ten or twelve
people in the Court Theatre who, with a blue pencil and a pair
of scissors, could turn Mr Shaw's play into a masterpiece. Why,
why, has he not always the respect for his own work which he
has for his own mind, his own soul, and his 'function'.

Some years ago the Stage Society performed two plays of
Chekov; *The Cherry Orchard* and *Uncle Vanya*. Of *Uncle
Vanya* I wrote in 1914, just before the war: 'The current of the
days is slow here, the air the characters breathe is sultry with
undischarged energy, and broken only by unrefreshing nerve
storms; it is an atmosphere of sighs and yawns and self-
reproaches, vodka, endless tea and endless discussion. But we
have no right to label this atmosphere 'Russian' and to regard it

with complacent curiosity. Have you not felt that fog in your throat on English lawns, in English houses? Indeed, the main point of difference between this spellbound cultivated Russian society and the English variety is not in our favour. If Chekov's intellectuals are half dead, the other half of them is very much and painfully alive. They suffer more consciously, there is intensity in their lassitude; at least they torture themselves and each other, by displaying each his own bankruptcy.' Now Mr Shaw, too, was apparently struck by this resemblance, and he proceeded to write a Tchekov play about English society. The result was a very remarkable one—*Heartbreak House*. Of course, his subject-matter was slightly different. English people are not like Russian people, but the great difference between such a play as *Uncle Vanya* and *Heartbreak House* is due to the temperament of the author. Mr Shaw does not know what heartbreak is. He conceives it as a sudden disillusionment (*vide* his heroine), cauterising like a flash of lightning; as a sharp pain, but not as a maiming misery. Compared with the vital and restless inmates of *Heartbreak House* Chekov's characters are like dying flies in a glue-pot. He presents his play as an important diagnosis of real conditions, yet he allows his high spirits continually to turn it into farce, so that hardly one person in a hundred sees its relations to reality. But how excellent some scenes are, the opening of Act III for example.

LADY UTTERWORD. What a lovely night! It seems made for us.

HECTOR. The night takes no interest in us. What are we to the night? [*He sits down moodily in the deck chair.*]

ELLIE. [*Dreamily, nestling against the Captain*]. Its beauty soaks into my nerves. In the night there is peace for the old and hope for the young.

HECTOR. Is that remark your own?

ELLIE. No. Only the last thing the Captain said before he went to sleep.

CAPTAIN SHOTOVER. I'm not asleep.

HECTOR. Randall is. Also Mr. Mazzini Dunn. Mangan, too, probably.

MANGAN. No.

HECTOR. Oh, you are there. I thought Hesione would have sent you to bed by this time.

MRS. HUSHABYE [*coming to the back of the garden seat, into the light, with Mangan*]. I think I shall. He keeps telling me he has a presentiment that he is going to die. I never met a man so greedy for sympathy.

MANGAN [*plaintively*] But I have a presentiment. I really have. And you wouldn't listen.

MRS. HUSHABYE. I was listening for something else. There was a sort of splendid drumming in the sky. Did none of you hear it? It came from a distance and then died away.

MANGAN. I tell you it was a train.

MRS. HUSHABYE. And I tell you, Alf, there is no train at this hour. The last is nine forty-five.

MANGAN. But a goods train.

MRS. HUSHABYE. Not on our little line. They tack a truck on the passenger train. What can it have been, Hector?

HECTOR. Heaven's threatening growl of disgust at us useless futile creatures. [*Fiercely*] I tell you, one of two things must happen. Either out of that darkness some new creation will come to supplant us as we have supplanted the animals, or the heavens will fall in thunder and destroy us.

LADY UTTERWORD [*in a cool instructive manner, wallowing comfortably in her hammock*]. We have not supplanted the animals, Hector. Why do you ask heaven to destroy this house, which could be made quite comfortable if Hesione had any notion of how to live? Don't you know what is wrong with it?

HECTOR. We are wrong with it. There is no sense in us. We are useless, dangerous, and ought to be abolished.

This last remark of the vain, romancing, but (so we are given to understand) really gallant-spirited Hector annoys Lady Utterword, who maintains that what is wrong with 'the house' is merely the absence of horses. 'There are only two classes in good society in England: the equestrian classes and the neurotic classes. It isn't mere convention: everybody can see that the people who hunt are the right people, and the people who don't are the wrong ones.' This rather impresses the old Captain. Presently the melancholy flutings of the love-sick Randall are heard proceeding from a bedroom window. They start discussing whether Ellie ought to marry Mangan for his money. Mangan is induced to disclose the fact that though he is a millionaire he really owns nothing, a statement which is at first scoffed at. Lady Utterword suggests he should go in for politics, whereupon he indignantly exclaims that he *is* the dictator of a great public department, and he goes on to expatiate upon his administerial achievements, which seem to consist in preventing other heads of departments getting the glory of winning the war. From that the conversation passes to government. Lady Utterword thinks that the sooner the ridiculous shams of democracy are got rid of the better. If only we could be governed by Hastings (her husband) who, given a free hand and a plentiful supply of bamboo, would bring the British native to his senses. On this, the old Captain flashes out that any fool can govern with a stick in his hand, and that it is not God's way: 'The man is a numskull.' Ellie thinks her mild idealistic father would govern very well if only people would not cheat him and despise him because he is good, at which Mangan snorts with scorn. Mrs Hushabye says to Mangan: 'It matters very little who governs the country so long as we govern you.' 'Who is we, pray?' 'The devil's granddaughters, dear. The lovely women.' This makes the handsome Hector, who makes love mechanically one moment and regrets it the next, leap from his chair with balled fists; and then Ellie makes her little speech which is the key to the piece. She is a young girl whom Hector has bewitched, Othello-like, by his stories and vain-glorious poses. Her first shock was her discovery on coming to this house that her hero, 'Marcus Darnley', was really Hector Hushabye, her friend Hesione's husband. 'There seems to be nothing real in the world', she exclaims now, 'except my father and Shakespeare. Marcus' tigers are false; Mr Mangan's millions are false; there is nothing really strong and true about Hesione but her beautiful black hair; and Lady Utterword's is too pretty to be real. The one thing left me was the Captain's seventh degree of concentration, and that turns out to be'—Captain Shotover, interrupting—'Rum'. Lady Utterword deprecates the reference to her own hair; a good deal of it, she says, is genuine, but, of course, the colour is not natural. This is too much for Mangan, who has been tortured and bewildered by this atmosphere of candour. He starts taking off his coat, roaring: 'What shame is there in this house? Let's all strip naked.' 'How are we to have any self respect,' he whimpers, 'if we don't keep it up that we are better than we really are?' He will go back to the city where he is respected and made much of. Then in the semi-darkness of the garden we hear a chorus of mocking goodbyes, 'Good-bye, Alf, think of us sometimes. Think of Ellie's youth. Think of Hesione's eyes and hair!' 'Think of the garden', says the old man, 'in which you are not a dog barking to keep the truth out.' 'Think of Lady Utterword's beauty! Her good sense! Her style!' says Hector. 'Think, Mr Mangan', Lady Utterword adds, 'whether you can do any better for yourself elsewhere?' Mangan surrenders: he cannot leave this intellectual garden of Armide, for the attractions of *Heartbreak House* are by no means merely sensuous. When once you have tasted the delicious excitements of candour and free play of mind, all other society seems dull.

I have described and quoted from ten minutes of this remarkable play to show how well Mr Shaw has treated a group of people in the Chekov manner. It is a long play, but a packed one. He has telescoped throughout masses of emotion and observation into a few lines of dialogue. The characters are creations from an overflow of generalised experience, not merely individuals with a marked characteristic or two. They are typical as well as individual. The old Captain (a violent mystic), Mrs Hushabye, her worldly sister, Mazzini Dunn, the helpless idealist, are wonderfully drawn. Ellie Dunn, the young creature who is plunged into this roofless home, open to the speculation of the stars and all the winds of opinion, where she learns in an afternoon more about life than she might have picked up in ten years, and whose reactions enable us to diagnose its atmosphere, is a very inferior creation. So are Boss Mangan and Hector. In the case of Ellie, Mr Shaw's sentimentality has run away with him, and in the case of the two latter characters his high spirits. In spite of the masterly concision of some of the dialogue, the play is too long. In spite of the fact that Mr Shaw found he had more to hint at and define than he could manage, he had loaded his play with foolery which is not only unnecessary, but fatal to securing the effects he wants to make. He introduces a comic mesmeric scene and a spoof burglar, who turns out to be an ex-pirate known to the Captain and also the runaway husband of the housekeeper. Does he expect (I cannot help writing as though I were shouting at him) us to be amused by that tomfoolery? Or if we are, that we can then maintain the mood necessary to feel the tragi-comedy of these fine people (for each in his or her way, except Mangan, have something in them), whose disease is not due to the absence of horse-exercise, but to the absence of a clear aim in life and a sense of proportion? Everything in them has consequently run, as in Chekov's plays, to talk. Mr Shaw is gloriously an artist in his sense of the importance of ideas, and in his sense of a subject, but he is without artistic respect for unity of effect. It seems he does not care about it. He sows thistles for donkeys in his flower beds, and then wonders at the donkeys for munching them and trampling on the flowers. His high spirits are a wonderful gift, but they master and distract him, and they have seriously damaged this fine play.

What was the point of making Mangan and the burglar perish in the air raid? A bit of symbolism? It was a stupid one. A bit of fun? It was not funny, and made the closing words unreal. The production was not satisfactory; the conversational pitch was too often broken by shouting. It was vital that these people who were fantastic but real, should behave, superficially, as conventionally as possible. No restraint, however, was put upon them. Still Mr Brember Wills's Captain Shotover was admirable, also Miss Edith Evans' Lady Utterword.

CHEKHOV AND SHAW

April 3, 1943

'A FANTASY IN the Russian manner on English themes'—that is the descriptive sub-title of *Heartbreak House*, published in 1919, first performed in October 1921. Technically this play was the result of the impact of Chekhov upon Shaw the dramatist; in substance it was a work begotten upon his contempt for cultured, leisured, pre-fourteen England by—his jocular despair. It was begun before the unforeseen, undreamt of catastrophe of 1914, but finished, as the last act shows, in the midst of it. He held it back because he thought that it revealed what it was not expedient to expose while the issue was still in the balance; and when 'the Germans', as he wrote in the preface, 'might on any night have turned the last act from play to earnest, and even then might not have waited for their cues.' This objection, of course, if ever sound, would apply more forcibly now. True, the youthful heroine's cry for bombs and more bombs, on which the curtain falls, wakes no responsive echo in our hearts today, but the audience manifested no desire to hoot. Nor have I spoken yet with anyone who considered that the picture presented of upper-class fecklessness and the idotic egotism of business bosses in wartime could shake national morale. On the contrary the audience evidently enjoyed themselves thoroughly without misgivings. And no wonder. When *Heartbreak House* is as well performed as it is at the Cambridge Theatre, it is one of the most excitingly amusing and interesting of Shaw's plays. This is the best performance of it I have seen, including that of the Pitoeffs in Paris, both for individual acting (passages in certain parts present almost insuperable difficulties) and production and scenery. Miss Deborah Kerr as

Ellie Dunn, Mr Robert Donat as Captain Shotover, Mr George Merrit as Boss Mangan (equally excellent at moments of arrogance, bewilderment or deflation), Mr J. H. Roberts as Mazzini Dunn (an easier part, granted a temperamental turn for portraying mild sincerity), achieved a high distinction in their parts. The gestures and elocution of Miss Edith Evans (Hesione Hushabye) showed, as might be expected, a delightful comprehension of the part. Her acting was a triumph for the artist, but the woman could not sustain completely the role of an elderly but ever-young enchantress (Hesione, among Shaw's creations, is the last gleam of his love for Ellen Terry). Miss Isabel Jeans's fashionable languor as Lady Utterword left little to be desired. Her confident and self-consciously poised voice perfectly suited the part, but I have a warning to give her; in looking after her pellucidly musical intonations, her articulation was apt to become indistinct. I was not far from the stage, yet some of her words escaped me. Hector Hushabye is one of those parts which it is impossible to unify completely. Mr Vernon Kelso achieved what is possible in that direction by wisely keying down the acting of it, while his prosaic but dressy stolidity contrasted amusingly with the fantastic romanticism of that caricature. The tiny part of Nurse Guinness, which provides a spot of the normal in a world of eccentrics, and that of the over-simplified rotter, Randall, were well filled by Miss Amy Veness and Mr Francis Lister. No actor in the world could make the Burglar significant, but Mr Philip Godfrey strove splendidly to suggest that he was meant to be funny. The whole burglar episode is certainly a mistake—certainly the identification of him with the ex-pirate and the long-lost husband of Nurse Guinness is a false note. Such incidents belong to the world of farce. Although Bernard Shaw's high-spirited agility in modulating out of serious and even poetic comedy into intellectual farce is one of his astonishing stage-gifts, he sometimes abuses it. I think he has done so here.

There! I have mentioned the whole cast, which a critic

never does unless their playing together has been more than satisfactory. In one respect Miss Kerr may be said to prop up the whole play, for she is the only 'Ellie' whose acting and personality have been as yet sympathetic and vivid enough to enable us to ignore the thundering impossibility of her sudden transformation from a chit of a girl green enough to swallow Hector's stories, into an acute, collected woman capable of exposing Mangan to himself and playing cat to his mouse. Much is said about 'heartbreak' in the course of this play, and the characters in it seem to be valued according to the degree in which they have, thanks to it, approached a salutary dis-illusionment—topped, of course, by the old captain himself, who has very nearly become one of those 'who are so sufficient to themselves that they are only happy when they are stripped of everything, even of hope.' But, maturing as the shock may be for a girl in her teens to suddenly discover that her day-dream lover (an acquaintance who had enchanted her with stories of his daring) is married to her friend and an incorrigible liar, it would need more than that to make her discard all hope of love, all reliance on human nature. Only disillusionment in a relation where body and heart had been involved and emotions passionately reciprocated, or where some deep common aim had been betrayed, could possibly lead to such detachment as is indicated by Ellie's cry 'I feel now as if there were nothing I could not do because I *want nothing*', and to the old man's comment, 'That's the only real strength. That's the only real strength. That's genius.' What has Ellie actually suffered? An excruciating humiliation on finding that her superb 'Marcus Darnley' was only Mr Hushabye! The discovery made her exclaim 'I'm damning myself for being such a fool.' It was in the right key; her later exclamation was not.

The love, and therefore also the kind of disillusionment, the kind of pain, which could alone have led to a conversion to the selfless life through 'heartbreak', is nowhere represented in Shaw's drama. Love of the fancy, such as Ellie's, is there—gay, or silly, or wild-spirited; comradeship touched with childish humour because it is affection between man and woman, is there; sex-attraction indicated, but only as an impulse isolated from the emotional life of those concerned as completely as a trance under laughing-gas. The love that could account for Ellie's desolation never appears. Of course, if the dramatist had made Hushabye seduce her (and he is a man who, when embracing his sister-in-law, cannot resist a lustful kiss) . . . but who can imagine anything so painful, so unpleasant, occurring in a Shaw play as the seduction of a charming child by an elderly boaster! It would be intolerable to his sensitive delicacy to base a psychological situation on anything so ugly. He would far rather cook it as he has done.

When you come to think of it, does anything really painful ever occur on his stage? His themes may be ostensibly tragic or unpleasant—judged by the intellect—but by his treatment of them the impact on us of what is painful is muffled. Death occurs, but is it ever painful? True there was St. Joan, but history wrote that story; and Shaw was careful to explain that it was not in the agonies of the Maid, but in the fact that the world was unworthy of her that the tragedy lay. I cannot recall a moment of devastating grief for another in any of his plays; I cannot recall a single bad character in them who makes an impression, frightening or revolting, of evil. Mangan in this play is described as vermin that should be exterminated; he is condemned as socially and economically noxious. But in himself Mangan is not revolting; he is merely stupid, childish and even amiable. Bernard Shaw's drama is life depicted with the detachment of the Comic Spirit, not with the tragic detachment of one who has come through to the other side of suffering. It is the art of one who has seen, and seen very clearly, horrors and predicaments, but hardly felt them deeply. I hope some readers noticed a phrase I used at the beginning of this article—'his jocular despair.'

I gather from Mr E. Strauss's admirable book, *Bernard*

Shaw's Art and Socialism that the dramatist himself even regards *Heartbreak House*, together with *Back to Methuselah*, as his greatest artistic achievement. I have not been able to trace such a passage, but I emphatically disagree with it. *Back to Methuselah* is his most ambitious achievement, a very different thing; and *Heartbreak House*, in spite of its rare merits (he has never orchestrated dialogue better) is zig-zagged by a flaw from top to bottom.

It purports to be a picture of the upper-class intelligentsia of England during the first world war; of an English country-house group corresponding in futility to Chekhov's characters in *The Cherry Orchard* and *Uncle Vanya*, I repeat, in wartime. And there lies the flaw. As a picture of behaviour and talk in an English country house during the summer of nineteen-fifteen or sixteen or seventeen, or whenever the action is supposed to take place, the play has no relation to reality. Whatever cogency it might have had as an exposure of the fecklessness of the cultured upper-class in England before the war, at the time when the characters and situations were conceived by the dramatist, has been falsified by his post-dating it in order to exhibit Nemesis in the form of falling bombs. Neither the denizens of *Heartbreak House*, nor those of Horseback Hall, behaved like the characters in this play when the catastrophe came. On the contrary their sons, in a spirit that was half joy of life, half willingness to die, volunteered at once; their women (enjoying themselves, but that is neither here nor there) ran hospitals and did war work. Why, this particular group would never have assembled under the roof of Captain Shotover at all! The byronic Hushabye, so nauseated by an existence that made no demands on his devotion and courage that he lived in absurd day-dreams of romantic prowess, always seized every chance of risking his life, and now actually turns on the lights in defiance, when German planes are overhead—to him the war would have been a godsend. He would have got to the front long before. Lady Utterword, with cool, high-handed serenity, would be running a hospital in France. And can't I see Hesione dispensing coffee and charm at two in the morning to dazed, frozen, sleep-starved men at Boulogne station night after night; giving the glad-eye to generals and tommies alike, thus reawakening in them, though she may have a middle-age spread, that love of life which is so necessary to soldiers who have to die? Mazzini Dunn would be standing up, not to bullets, but to rotten eggs, as a pacifist and member of the Union of Democratic Control; and his daughter Ellie, torn between her devotion to him and her longing for activity, would either be singing to the troops at Poperinghe or driving a car behind the lines. Yes, in actuality, the Ancient Mariner would have been left alone in his house, drinking his rum and brooding over his destructive invention and his bitter, brave old soul; growing even more convinced since war began that civilisation was hopeless. The floods may be out, but Oh! who will torpedo the Ark? Perhaps Captain Shotover-Ibsen-Shaw?

Yet after all, what superb qualities the play has! Captain Shotover is one of Shaw's finest character-creations. Into him he has put what lies deep, though disguised, in him, his lack of faith in man. Again, here, for once he has created 'atmosphere . This is the air which circulates in a ramshackle Palace of Truth and affects all who breathe it. Here lies the charm, the fun, the excitement of the play for us also. Under Captain Shotover's roof all barriers are down, all wigs are off, everyone speaks out of himself or herself. How embarrassing and painful for those not used to such an atmosphere, but for others what a relief! So that we, too, as we leave, feel like Ellie about it: 'This silly house, this strangely happy home, this agonising house, this house without foundations. I shall call it Heartbreak House.'

GETTING MARRIED

April 8, 1922

L AST WEEK *Getting Married* was revived at the Everyman
Theatre, Hampstead. After an interval of fourteen years I am
going to criticise it as though it were a new play, because
at the time of its first production it was not thoroughly criticised.
Mr Shaw's dramatic reputation had just reached that dangerous
point when his admirers felt it needed no further championing
and the play was a disappointment. Mr Duffin (*The
Quintessence of Bernard Shaw*), and others who have written
books about him, have dealt admirably with the ideas the play
contains, but as a dramatic entertainment it has received
scanty comment.

Getting Married, described by its author as 'a disquisitory
play', is an animated conversation upon our marriage laws
and customs, which naturally involves a discussion of sex and
human needs, and the views different people take of those needs
in their neighbours. There is no dramatic progression, and little
dialectical progress is made, though the trend of the argument
on practical reforms is clear: divorce is not the destruction of
marriage but the first condition of its maintenance; therefore
make it as easy, as cheap, as private as marriage; sexual relations
between men and women will not be decent and honourable
until women are economically independent; as a first step,
place the work of a wife and a mother on the same footing as
other work. However socially important these conclusions may
be, the incidents and the talk concerned with them are not the
most interesting parts of the play. The play is all talk; but it is
brilliant talk, which starts many hares, and throws light on
human nature; and however serious in intention the dialogue
is rampageously gay. Although there is no development, a
mild emotional tension is created by the temporary refusal of a

young couple to get married a few hours before the ceremony, having just had their attention drawn to the terrifying legal aspects of the contract they were about to make; and a further tension is created by the presence among the wedding guests of an elderly uncle of the bride, who has just had a decree *nisi* pronounced against him (the action was collusive), and also by his meeting his young wife and the young man for whose sake she wanted to be divorced. There is yet a third emotional element, and therefore a possible source of dramatic interest, in the presence of a married woman who has inspired in this young man one of those fantastic, sudden, fatalistic passions with which Mr Shaw's drama, rather than life itself, has made us familiar; while she, Mrs George, nourishes a distant adoration for the Bishop, the father of the bride, the idealising nature of which passion she understands herself so well that she hoped never to meet him, except in heaven. These 'situations' are not, however, there for the sake of their dramatic possibilities; they form, as it were, a revolving pedestal on which the statue of Marriage can be placed, which enables it to be exhibited to criticism from different angles. This criticism proceeds, not only from the people most concerned, but also from others (types created from an overflow of observation and amusingly exaggerated), who either from temperament or prejudice only see one aspect of love and marriage. It is our business, of course, to weigh their miscellaneous comments: some of these seem pointful till a twist is given to the statue on the pedestal; others seem to hold good despite that, and others are only interesting as indications of character. Here Mr Shaw's gift for making people speak out of themselves and lending them, for that purpose, his own smiting directness of speech tells magnificently. We are kept alert and amused. I have laid bare the structure of the play because these discussion plays are thought to be 'formless', and the skill with which Mr Shaw constructs them has escaped notice. The justification of this type of play is that it enables a writer to cover far more of a

large subject than can be illustrated in the space of three hours
by action alone. It has its own form, a different one, and
Mr Shaw is master of it.

The first production, fourteen years ago, must have been
excellent, for I found myself comparing the Everyman actors
and actresses, adequate as many were, to their predecessors
in their parts, as though I had known these characters in the
flesh. Mr Milton Rosmer suffered in comparison with Mr
Ainsworth in the part of St John Hotchkiss, Mr Felix Aylmer
with Mr Ainley as the Bishop; for, although good, Mr Aylmer
was a little too drily charmless, and he lacked the unction of a
very amiable nature—but I need not go through the list. Only
Soames (Father Antony) had, it seemed to me, found now an
even better interpreter in Mr Hignett. It is an actor-proof part,
but Mr Hignett made it really human; his appearance, too, was
perfect; ascetic in countenance, in figure resembling an alpaca
umbrella-case.

This play contains a number of parts which act themselves;
one which requires high spirits raised almost to the pitch of
genius (Hotchkiss), and one which it is impossible to act,
(Mrs George Collins). Hotchkiss is first cousin to Tanner and
half brother to Valentine and Charteris; perhaps I should not
have understood, though I should certainly have enjoyed him,
if I had not known his relations. But I cannot pull Mrs
George together in imagination, nor, so far as I remember,
could Miss Fanny Brough in 1908, nor can Miss Gertrude
Kingston now in 1922, though she spoke excellently well the
trance speeches, in which the Eternal Feminine is supposed
to give us through her mouth a piece of its mind. I conclude
it is the author's fault; that he has not created a character,
but just flung together with immense assurance fragments of
a virago, a *grande dame*, Joan (wife of Darby), a pantomime
wit, George Sand, and a mystic. Though she says some
interesting things, and interesting things are said about her, she
is not intelligibly alive—devastatingly prominent, but not a

human being. It is curious to notice how indefinite in some respects Mr Shaw is about her. She is, for instance, first described to us by her brother-in-law as a woman 'that changeable and what you might call susceptible, you would not believe.' When she fell in love she had no control over herself; but according to Collins, men invariably ran away from her or brought her back to her husband; although she is supposed to have exhausted all forms of amorous experience, her disillusionments appear then to have been of a monotonous character. She seems to be a confirmed Platonist, valuing love for the visions and aspirations it inspires. Her trance speech 'when you loved me I gave you the whole sun and stars to play with. I gave you eternity in a single moment. . . . Must I mend your clothes and sweep your floors as well? . . . I gave you your own soul: you asked for my body as a plaything. Was it not enough?' is Platonic in its philosophy. The speech lacks emotional rhythm and verbal magic. Why 'the whole' sun, for instance? The symbol, too, is commonplace. Mr Shaw does not rise in diction to the height of his conception here.

Mr Shaw has usually represented the state of being in love as a state of wild high spirits, so irrational that in the wide-awake male it awakens terror, and he has attempted to dignify it by dwelling on its generative purpose. This little breath of Platonism is certainly refreshing in his work, though it is immediately vulgarised. We are also confused at the end by Mrs George's seeming assent to Father Antony's phrase, 'Christian fellowship', as the description of what every woman really wants; a rare, beautiful, but quite different thing.

In Hotchkiss we see once more, as in so many scenes in Mr Shaw's plays, passion represented in terms of extravagant farce. It would be amusing and satisfactory if at the same time we had not the uncomfortable feeling that we are meant, also, to take him seriously, too. In the love scenes between Mrs George and Hotchkiss, in which she takes the poker to him and bites, there is an exaggeration of an element often present in

Mr Shaw's love scenes: the infatuation of the man is represented as heightened by the dominating violence of the woman, just as in normal and commonplace drama the woman is often represented as being fascinated by the roughness and brutality of the man. It has little or nothing in common with Petruchio's admiration of Kate when in a fury she rages up and down the room.

> Did ever Dian so become a grove
> As Kate this chamber with her princely gait?

These scenes between Hotchkiss and Mrs George seem to me deplorable; too funny to be serious, and too serious to be funny.

MISALLIANCE

A NOTE

November 8, 1924

MISALLIANCE IS NOT one of Mr Shaw's best plays, but it is exceedingly interesting. It may be regarded in a measure as a preliminary canter for the far finer *Heartbreak House*. The theme is not the same, but the method is, and the share contributed by the comic burglar in the latter, and the homicidal clerk in *Misalliance* (his motives are more interestingly treated, by the bye, in *Captain Brassbound*), is the same. Some of the ideas, too, in *Misalliance* recur in *Heartbreak House* and in *Methuselah*, only in a context which makes them much more significant. *Misalliance* is a discussion play. It is an extremely vivacious and absorbing discussion, centering on the relations between youth and age, and between parents and children in particular. But vivacious, amusing and amazingly acute as the discussion is, the critic feels that Mr Shaw when he wrote the play, had not a clear notion where his perceptions in this case were leading him. It is inconclusive. The play is one of those works which occur periodically in the life-work of every author who keeps pushing along, which are the expression of a period when his mind is at pause. It has the defects of such works. We have the idea presented that to grow old is to become more spiritualised and more delicate in feeling and judgment, which, of course, is the beginning of the idea on which *Back to Methuselah* stands. But in *Misalliance* the playwright, if anything, takes the side of youth, graceless, crude, insensitive youth. All that clearly emerges is that the elderly cannot manage, help or guide the young, and that the parental relation is a drawback to making some sort of a success of education. The young man who is represented as the most satisfactorily equipped specimen of youth (I do not think the allegorical and impossible figure of the female-super-acrobat, Lina, counts as a character at all) is 'Percival', who was brought up by three fathers. The wish of the old Lord Summerhays to love and cherish the young Hypatia is shown to be foolish, and the helplessness and bewilderment of Tarleton (the best character in the play) as a father, is presented as a proof of the hopelessness of parental education. In Tarleton, in his vital, impetuous abruptness, I thought I recognised the rudiments of the fascinaing and wonderful old Captain Shotover (*Heartbreak House*), only, of course, he is not a mystic who has pulled the world together in his head, but an impetuous dunderhead with a heart of gold. Mr Clark played him well at the Everyman Theatre; indeed, his performance was the best and most amusing of the whole cast. Mr Barnard was not the right type for the part of Bentley; he struggled manfully with it, but he naturally could not get rid of his personality. There are some extremely acute observations in the dialogue upon the crippling shyness which exists between parents and children worth going a long way to listen to, but the general drift of the play towards the conclusion that the relation between parents and children is a mistake, and had better be scrapped, is not very helpful. The play is not one of Mr Shaw's masterpieces, but it exhibits his extraordinary power of blending the utterly fantastic with piercing insight into fact, and of making discussion so amusing that on the stage it throws most comedies of situation in the shade as an entertainment.

ST JOAN

THE THEME

April 5, 1924

S T *JOAN* IS a play of many and splendid merits. It is
immensely serious and extremely entertaining; it is a
magnificent effort of intellectual energy and full of pathos
and sympathy; it is long but it never flags; it is deep, and I am
by no means sure that I have got, or that I am going to get, to
the bottom of it; it is a play it would be disgraceful to treat
inadequately—I shall return to it next week. I intend now to
make only a few preliminary remarks. We are lifted on waves
of emotion to be dashed on thought. Only a languid mind
could fail to find in it intellectual excitement, only a very
carefully protected sensibility could escape being touched and
disturbed—but I must add a proviso to that. The theme of the
play is religion; therefore to be touched and disturbed by it
in any appreciable degree the spectator, some time or other,
must have experienced religious emotions himself; and further,
having done so, he must not loathe them as some people loathe
amorous emotions after having been dipped in them. He may
distrust religious emotion, dislike exceedingly many of its
manifestations (as, indeed, I do myself), but he must know what
kind of a feeling it is and how it can draw and drag at the heart;
otherwise he will neither apprehend the whole, nor feel the
force of its most dramatic moments.

Of course much remains which a spectator who lacked such
experience could and would enjoy; but *St Joan* is not a
chronicle play. It is not primarily an historic drama. It is a
religious play. Mr Shaw, needless to say, has a very powerful
and dramatic imagination, but the historic side of it is not the
strongest. Has he a love of the past? I believe he would scout

the idea. The question would seem to him equivalent to asking
him if he had a love of bric-à-brac. I do not believe he cares a
dump for things that are dead, gone and changed. The first
thing he invariably does when his setting is in the past, is to
rub off his period the patina of time (*vide* Cæsar and Cleopatra);
he will scrub and scrub till contemporary life begins to gleam
through surface strangenesses and oddities. He is confident
that he has reached historic truth when he has succeeded in
scratching historic characters till he finds beneath a modern
man in fancy dress. He is careful of historic facts in this play;
he never introduces anything equivalent to making Cleopatra
play billiards; but the play is full of spiritual anachronisms.
The atmosphere is not that of the Middle Ages. Let me give
some examples: when Joan is told that her voices are the work
of her imagination, she replies, 'God speaks to us through our
imaginations.' No idea could be more foreign to the Middle
Ages than that, or more typical of the latest modern religious
'heresy', of which Mr Shaw himself is the exponent. Again,
the Earl of Warwick is a purely eighteenth century nobleman;
he is not even a Renaissance character. I think he is closely
related to General Burgoyne. The delightful study of a common
English type, Warwick's clerical secretary, is brother of our
old friend Britannicus—of the Bishop of London, and many a
shell-making patriotic parson. But does all this matter? To
my mind not a bit. It merely substitutes another kind of interest,
and one, too, closer to the emotions of the majority of people.
Mr Shaw would jump at the definition of his St Joan as 'a
modern heretic'. I can fancy him saying: 'Why, trying to pick a
hole in my work you have blundered on my central point.' I
know I have. Twice in the course of the play Joan is defined as
'a Protestant'. The essence of Protestantism is that the
authority of the individual's religious experience is final for
him. No matter if disagreement and chaos result, it is the
highest duty of everyone to obey, like Joan, his 'Voices'. He
must listen attentively, he must live so as to sharpen his

hearing; but when he is sure of what they say he must obey. God does not speak through tradition or organised religions, but is resident in the hearts and minds of men. In fact what we call our hearts, our minds, are, according to Mr Shaw, the spirit of God Himself, a baffled, disturbed, struggling but inevitably emerging force, and—this is the accompanying emotion of such convictions and the source of their consoling and sustaining power—a force necessarily triumphant in the end. The confusion of voices does not matter; it is inevitable. In so far as the voices are genuine they are efforts, some of them perhaps futile, of the Spirit of the Universe itself to find a way. The first duty of man is to make himself a channel for its passage. If he does so he is a 'saint', and though he may be burned, he will have a strange power even over those who burn him or mock him. And what is the test of 'genuineness'? That is the crux. Organised religions say—we and our traditions; the statesman says the test is, do these saints or do they not threaten the social order; the people, whether they do or do not protest against our tyrants; the nationalist, whether they do or do not inspire patriotism; the soldier, whether they do or do not make for victory; the Gallios, whether they do or do not make for pleasure and peace. The Church is prepared to accept a canonised Joan once her dynamic and incalculably disruptive force has spent itself or been destroyed; while the fairer of its spokesmen are prepared to admit, even as they condemn her, that she may be better and more religious than themselves; the statesman that she is far from ignoble; the soldier that she alone could put the right spirit into fighting men, and they are ready to use her as long as desperate courage is a means to victory. But none of them want her back.

Joan, or rather the spirit within her, is shown in conflict with each of these powers and different points of view, and this conflict is the essence of the drama. But I must repeat for the sake of emphasis that this is not primarily an historical play. It is the tragedy of Joan herself of course as well, of a real girl whom we see before our eyes, who did the things we hear of on the stage, who triumphed, then failed and was burnt. But its central theme is wider; it is the struggle of religious inspiration against the world, down the ages, which, Mr Shaw would assert, was always essentially the same struggle, whether the world's antagonist is Jesus, Joan, Huss, Galileo, or one of the many lesser men and women. It is a struggle which cannot be won in any complete sense and yet can never be lost. The spiritual and intellectual anachronisms are therefore in a sense artistic merits, for they help to generalise the case. The last words are the cry of Joan as she appears in the King's dream, when each of her different opponents in turn acknowledges the beneficence of her inspiration, then wills that after all she shall never return again; 'O God, when will your world be fit for saints to live in.' She is left as alone as she was in her defeat, as alone as she was, in spite of appearances, in her victory.

The extraordinary intellectual merit of this play is the force and fairness with which the case of her opponents is put; the startling clarity with which each of them states it, and consequently our instantaneous recognition of its relation to the religious instinct. One of Mr Shaw's most remarkable gifts has always been this rare generosity. It is odd, but he has never drawn a wicked character—plenty of characters who do wicked things, but not one wicked man. He has never believed in the devil, only in blindness, inertia and stupidity; faults so widely spread it seems a failure of common sense to distinguish particular people by special abhorrence.

The other extraordinary merit of the play is the intensity of its religious emotion and the grasp the dramatist shows of the human pathos of one who is filled with it, as well as showing his or her immunity from requiring anything like pity. It is probably I think, the greatest of Shaw's plays. How these qualities are brought out, how the dramatist has put his theme in perspective and how his intentions were interpreted I will discuss next week.

April 12, 1924

THERE IS NO longer any doubt about the reception of this play. Last week I reserved all discussion of its dramatic qualities and the acting, and confined myself to an exposition of its theme. One point, however, I must repeat before adding further comments. The object of the play is to show Joan, or rather the spirit within her, in conflict with those who at first make use of her and then destroy her, and although the tragedy we watch is the tragedy of the girl we see before our eyes, who has a close resemblance to the real saint (though it is not hard to imagine a closer), the aim of the play is not primarily a reconstruction of the past, nor its primary aim to move us to pity. As the epilogue, to which several dramatic critics have objected, shows, the essence of the theme is the struggle of religious inspiration against established religions, against the patriot, the statesman and the indifferent—above all, against the Catholic Church, the strongest of them. In a sense the play can be described as an exceedingly powerful Protestant pamphlet, the essence of Protestantism being reliance upon internal authority (Joan's faith in her Voices) as against the authority of tradition and a corporate religion which also claim inspiration. Mr Shaw states the case of the Church through the mouths of the Bishop of Beauvais (admirably acted by Mr Eugene Leahy), the Inquisitor and the Archbishop of Rheims (Mr Robert Cunningham's ecclesiastical aplomb and deportment are perfect) with extraordinary fairness. Although the spectacle of the heresy-hunters in the trial scene is painful and odious in the last degree, the gentleness of the Inquisitor's address adding a peculiarly sinister quality to it, the speeches of both the Bishop and the Inquisitor make it quite clear that they are not actuated by cruelty, but that the Church itself is at stake in this argument. Joan must submit. The impulse of the sceptic is to shout 'So much the worse for the Church. If it can only preserve itself by torturing and burning a girl like Joan, in the name of everything that is good let it crumble and fall.' Both the Bishop and Inquisitor assert that in that case much worse barbarities, let alone utter confusion, would be let loose on the world. Mr Shaw presents their case, but because the play does not recall vividly the atmosphere of the Middle Ages, the strength of that case is hardly felt by the spectators. The mad credulity of the times is, it is true, suggested by the ease with which, in the first scene, the Sire de Baudricourt is convinced that Joan is inspired, for that the hens should begin to lay eggs as soon as he has granted her request to send her to the Dauphin with men at arms, is proof for him that her Voices are from God. In Scene 2 her recognition of the Dauphin, and in Scene 3, by the bank of the Loire, a sudden wished-for change of wind, has the same effect on others. What more, you may say, could Mr Shaw do in the short space allowed by a play? But the effect of these incidents on the atmosphere is neutralised by his peculiar dramatic method of making each character speak with a self-conscious awareness of the orientation of his own point of view, which is utterly foreign to the times. The method has enormous advantages, but it has that drawback. Further, none of these miracles suggest by their nature the vital importance of holding the fort of authority against heretics—they are harmless. To reinforce emotionally (intellectually Mr Shaw has done the Church ample justice) the case of Joan's persecutors, we could have been reminded with advantage of some of the horrors and absurdities which the hundreds of 'inspired' men and women were perpetually sacrificing their lives to propagate. Not many years after Joan's execution Gilles de Rais (he appears in Scene 2), under whose special protection the Maid was placed and who had won the name of a knight without fear or reproach, was attempting to get into touch with supernatural powers by cutting out the hearts and gouging out the eyes of innumerable children.

This, however, is minor criticism, for in the trial scene we are, after all, reminded by the speeches that the Church is engaged in a life and death struggle with paganism, witchcraft and State religion; only what has gone before has not made that fact as vivid as it might be. The only point at which it seemed to me a false note was struck was the moment when Joan recants her recantation. Her submission when faced with death is very moving, but when her sentence is changed to imprisonment for life she bursts out into a speech about nature and freedom, the hills and the sky, and tears up her recantation. This speech is the false note; to Joan the Mass and the Church were infinitely more important than lambs and larks or communion with nature. Mr Shaw has made her out more of a modern Protestant than any facts warrant. The speech, too, lacks that verbal beauty which alone could make it dramatically moving. The substance of poetry is often present in Mr Shaw's work (vide Scene 3, the kingfisher, the boy, and the general), but verbal magic never.

The most admirable and perfect scenes in the play are the two which immediately precede the trial scene, magnificent as that is, in spite of this one false note. They are discussions or conversations, and they are splendid examples of the critical truth that such scenes can contribute to dramatic effect as directly as scenes of action. Without them the trial scene would lose half its significance. In the first of them, the Earl of Warwick's tent in the English camp, the Earl and the Bishop of Beauvais decide the Maid's fate between them. Their reasons are bitterly antagonistic, and the point of view of the all-too-simple patriotic Englishman, Captain de Stogumber (Mr Lewis Casson played him to perfection, and Mr Lyall Swete as Warwick brought out the points of his part excellently), acts as a foil to these two subtle minds. The Bishop sees that Joan in her success has begun to act independently of the authority of the Church; the statesman that her mystic devotion to the King is a political heresy as dangerous to the real rulers of the land, the aristocracy. If the land belongs to the King, and the King is to give it to God and hold it for Him, where do the

168

great territorials come in? At the bottom of the religious nationalism of the Maid lies an appeal to the people. In Scene 5 in the ambulatory of Rheims Cathedral, after the coronation of the Dauphin, we see the Maid among her friends, who are soon to become her passive enemies. The archbishop reproves her for her independent pride—she is no longer the submissive daughter of the Church; the King wants to make a treaty with the English (God's enemies to Joan for the time being); the general, Dunois (Bastard of Orleans), explains to her that he knows exactly how much their own joint success has been due to her miraculous aid and how much to human agency and his own generalship. If she persists in moving on Paris in obedience to her Voices, he will not risk a single soldier's life to help her, or to save her. The time for reckless courage is over; he is grateful and admires her as a soldier, but she must be put aside as an instrument which has served its purpose. We know what is going to happen, of course, the tragedy which is to come. There is a fine dramatic irony therefore in these scenes, beside their effectiveness in bringing out the theme of the whole play—the conflict between religious emotion and the world. In the latter scene Miss Sybil Thorndike is at her very best. She is an actress with a very definite personality. It is difficult to judge, after seeing her, what latitude of interpretation the part actually allows. All that can be said is that her personality emphasises the insistive, energetic, almost pert traits in the Maid as Mr Shaw conceives her. Some of the critics and some of the public have refused to accept a Joan who calls the Dauphin 'Charlie', and shows so little superficial reverence for that semi-sacred personage. There is an excuse for this dramatic exaggeration. We know that the Maid 'theed' and 'thoued' the Dauphin and addressed him as *gentil Dauphin*, but that these peasant phrases and 'angelic familiarities' expressed the attitude of mind which Mr Shaw's paraphrases of them suggest, is doubtful. Still in any case the latter do convey what he wants to convey, the fearlessness and complete disregard of worldly estimates on the part of one who is filled with a divine mission. That the Maid sometimes answered her accusers with tartness is a fact, and Miss Thorndike does so most effectively; but the sweetness and simplicity of the Maid's replies and demeanour in the trial scene she does not bring out. Her distress, her alertness, her courage, she does drive home, but whether the fault lies in the part itself or in the interpretation, 'the angelic side' of the Maid is obscured. Mr Shaw so dreads the sentimental (when it is not a brusque denial of sentiment, itself sentimental), is so desirous that our response to beauty of character should be as ascetic as possible, that I am inclined to lay the blame on him in the first place, but there is no doubt that Miss Thorndike stresses this aversion to anything which might move us, first by its loveliness, only afterwards by its significance.

In a cast which is remarkable (and thanks to Mr Ricketts the costumes continually delight the eye), no part is more excellently played than the Dauphin (Mr Thesiger). I do not know enough history to check the portrait, but the one scene in which the Maid's power of inspiring others did not seem convincing was the dialogue between her and the Dauphin.

SAINTE JEANNE

June 21, 1930

THE INTERNATIONAL SEASON at the Globe Theatre, which we owe to Mr Cochrane and Mr Maurice Browne, is in full swing. On June 10 Georges and Ludmilla Pitoëff succeeded Moissi, whose performance of *Hamlet* I reviewed last week; and they in their turn will be followed by Japanese players.

During the war a small company of actors of different nationalities, aided by local amateurs, gave some performances in Geneva. M. Georges Pitoëff, a Russian of Armenian origin, and his Russian wife were the inspirers of this group. They were international in their choice of plays. Their repertory included plays by Shakespeare, Tolstoy and the French dramatist Lenormand, who had just begun to be known. This company, recruited by new talent, found its way to Paris, and there Mme Pitoëff became famous as an interpreter of parts which needed delicately natural and pathetic acting, and M. Pitoëff as a producer who left his stamp as an artist on every play he produced. Pirandello's *Six Characters in Search of an Author* was one of his first successes, and it was followed by a *Hamlet* which unfortunately cannot, owing to copyright difficulties, be performed here. With the exception of a French version of *Heartbreak House*, *Saint Joan* is the only Pitoëff production I have seen.

It is interesting to see what happens to a familiar play when it is transposed into another language and interpreted by foreign temperaments. Even when there is more loss than gain, this transposition may bring out more clearly the framework of a good drama. It is, indeed, a test whether or not the merits of a play lie only on the surface.

In the case of *Saint Joan* there were gains as well as losses, but those whose attention was arrested by surface peculiarities when the play was first produced, who were troubled about the historical accuracy of the general picture or by its intellectual anachronisms, will have learnt from seeing *Sainte Jeanne* how unimportant these points were, and that the play, in addition to being one of the very few fine religious plays in existence, is also intensely dramatic. The epilogue was, I remember, regarded by most critics and a large portion of the public as detracting from its impressiveness. I did not share that view. But either owing to the jokes in it seeming less prominent in translation, or to our having now recovered from the surprise of being let down after the tension of the final act, I should be surprised if the majority who attended the Globe Theatre last week were not struck, on the contrary, by its dramatic effectiveness and its congruity with the theme.

The subtle and pervasive change which the play underwent when re-interpreted by M. Pitoëff, and by his wife in the part of Jeanne, is easy to suggest: it was the elimination of its breeziness. I found that rather an improvement; for I enjoy Mr Shaw's breeziness more in his prefaces than in his plays. It is natural to compare these two actresses who have taken the leading part. Miss Sybil Thorndike is an actress with a definite personality, and her acting was so thorough that she became completely identified in my mind with Mr Shaw's Joan. It was very hard to judge after seeing her what latitude of interpretation the text actually allowed. Her personality emphasised the insistent, energetic, almost pert, traits in Joan as the dramatist had apparently conceived her, and she delivered her retorts effectively, most effectively; but in those moving records of the Maid's actual replies there is still perceptible a sweetness and simplicity which Miss Thorndike certainly did not bring out. Was it her fault or the dramatist's? Knowing his dread of sentiment and his determination that our response to beauty of character should be as ascetic and matter-of-fact as possible, I concluded that Miss Thorndike's interpretation was identical with his own. No one susceptible to the theme of the play, or to pathos, could have failed to be moved by moments in her acting, but in her interpretation of Saint Joan the 'angelic' side was eclipsed by a suggestion of the ardent public-spirited woman—in a word, there was more of Lady Astor about her than of a peasant who saw visions. After watching Mme Pitoëff I am inclined to think that Miss Thorndike was nearer to the part, and in one respect the twist she gave it was nearer, I thought, to historic reality. It was not so easy to imagine Mme Pitoëff's Sainte Jeanne as, for a time, forcing politicians, bishops and generals to do what she wanted, but more easy to imagine that her Saint Joan did so thanks to the magic of pure goodness rather than energy of character. Mme Pitoëff was far more pathetic. She was perhaps too much of a piteous little waif in her misery, and too much of a darling in armour at other moments to suggest completely the strange power of a saint. At one moment *Sainte Jeanne* seemed, certainly to foreign ears, a better play than *Saint Joan*, notably when she makes her recantation. It ends thus: 'I could do without my war-horse; I could drag about in a skirt; I could let the banners and the trumpets and the knights and the soldiers pass me and leave me behind as they leave other women, if only I could still hear the wind in the trees, the larks in the sunshine, the young lambs crying through the healthy frost, and the blessed, blessed church bells that send my angel voices floating to me on the wind. But without these things I cannot live; and by your wanting to take them away from me, or from any human creature, I know that your counsel is of the devil, and that mine is of God.'

Mr Shaw cannot get poetry into his words. He has supreme gifts as a dramatist, insight and invention, generosity and fearlessness of mind; but when he calls upon the Muse of Words to do more for him than to define and state, she does not answer. Notice how dramatically strong the last statement is, and how full of excruciating false notes the passages which precede it are. 'Drag about in a skirt' . . . 'the young lambs crying through the healthy frost', etc. Good heavens! This is the voice not of Jeanne d'Arc but of a suffragette and a cry from a garden city. 'Healthy frost!' Where has his imagination flown to? No mediaeval shepherdess would think the frost healthy. Well, in *Sainte Jeanne* these false notes, this poor diction, were partially veiled from English ears.

There was one bad mistake in the production of the trial scene, and M. Pitoëff seems to have temporarily lost his sense of the appropriate. When Jeanne utters unconsciously an enormous heresy the whole conclave turned their backs upon her and remained for several minutes with their faces covered by their sleeves. Now, in a scene which depends for its significance and poignancy upon its immediate suggestion of reality, this sort of drilled spectacular movement runs counter to the spirit of it.

The French Inquisitor was inferior to our English one. The spectacle of the heresy-hunters is painful and odious in the last degree, and the gentleness of the Inquisitor's address, the genuine compassion in it, reveals what is deeper, the irony of the situation. That speech makes clear that the heresy-hunters are not cruel, but that in this argument the Church—her Authority—is at stake. The dramatic point of the scene before our eyes—and also the point which is presented to our understanding—is that it should force us to cry, 'So much the worse, then, for the Church if it can only preserve itself by torturing a girl like Joan', and also make us aware of the other side. Mr Shaw had had barely time to suggest the mad credulity of the time. His historic sense, too, is limited to interpreting the past in terms of the present, a method which reveals much in it but far from all, for human characteristics do change. As I have said, to make us aware emotionally of the Church's full case, the play would have had to show us something of the horrors and absurdities which many men and women in those days were perpetually sacrificing their lives to propagate. The dramatist has not had time to *show* against what a chaos of superstition Authority was the only bulwark; but he has put the statement of the dangers of heresy—of a belief in direct inspiration—into the mouths of the Inquisitor and the Bishop of Beauvais. The speech of the Inquisitor must therefore be given emphatic space in the trial scene. It is as important as Joan's replies. In the French version it was delivered with a legal perfunctoriness. Thus the balance, which is so fine a part, not only of that scene, but of the play, was lost. And it was all the more important that the speech should not have been perfunctory because the part of the Bishop was played with a splendid peremptory harshness, in itself quite in keeping, but rendering more than ever necessary the gentle implacable truth of the Inquisitor's attitude—if the persecutors were to be seen and judged by the audience as the dramatist intended. Mr Shaw has written much that has made me respect him profoundly, but nothing makes me respect him more than this play, in which he, who as a religious man trusts the experience of the individual as final, has been impeccably fair to organised religion and left his saint as lonely in her posthumous triumph as she was in her defeat.

OVER-RULED

THE GAIETY OF BERNARD SHAW

August 13, 1927

INSIDE MR SHAW there plays perpetually a little fountain of irrational gaiety: I am inclined to think it is his distinguishing characteristic as a writer. I call this gaiety of spirit 'irrational' because it is quite unaffected by his conclusions or by events. How refreshing it is in hot debate we know, how cooling to the swollen solemnity of passion, how exhilarating to watch! (I prefer myself to drink courage at a spring of laughter than to get 'dutch courage' from a swig at anger's brandy bottle, though the temporary glow obtained be deeper and more delicious). However black the views Mr Shaw may be expressing—and his darker thoughts might arm a row of pessimists—however grave his theme, however urgent the controversy in which he is engaged, however disappointing public events, however personal the attacks upon himself, however saturated with private sorrow the subject he handles (I remember the scandal of his comments upon the foundering of the *Titanic*), that little fountain never ceases to play. For years this temperamental peculiarity puzzled the public, but the quality of a man's lifework will tell in the end, and few regard him now as an irresponsible jester; while many have found that if they press where they see that 'white plume shine amid the ranks of war', though they may occasionally find themselves dashing against impregnable positions, they have never been led upon an unchivalrous or selfish crusade. The white plume of the fountain was just as evident in the days when he wrote as an economic reformer as it was when he was basing his hopes for the future on the idea of breeding a superior race and as it was when he discovered later that, if progress was

176

to be possible, men must also learn to live to be thousands of years old. His notions have continually changed, but the gaiety of his spirit has never altered or faltered. It is the most permanent element in his response to life. Being intellectually cautious to the point of scepticism myself, and unable to see sufficient evidence round me to support the theory of 'the Life Force', I am inclined to read his conversion to that religion as an attempt to rationalise this indomitable and fortunate temperamental peculiarity in himself; as though he had asked himself: 'Whence springs this gaiety and courage of mine which survives everything, if not from a deep intuition concerning the nature of things? How else could I, who care about the welfare of humanity, enjoy this gay freedom of the spirit while fighting its doubtful battles?' To me the prefaces of Bernard Shaw are delightful and stimulating because they unite the ardour of the preacher with not a few of the virtues of detachment.

All this may seem remote from dramatic criticism, yet it subtends upon a point which struck me while watching the performance at the Everyman Theatre last week to which I shall presently turn. *Over-ruled* preceded the performance of Strindberg's *The Father*. *Over-ruled* is a trifling item in Mr Shaw's dramatic works, a trifle which it is impossible to read without amusement and instruction, but one which can fall (as we saw) most dismally flat upon the stage. The fact is that 'Shaw' is much more difficult to act than producers and actors grasp. In the first place, his technique is as far removed from realism as eighteenth-century technique. His characters seldom speak words they would actually utter; each says instead the things most typical of his or her point of view. In old days when Mr Shaw was defending his own work, he used to reiterate that his characters were so real that only a public accustomed to mere puppets would not recognise them as such. The defence was both sound and unsound. The surface of his drama often corresponds less to immediately recognisable actualities than the poorest society play, but the situations beneath that artificial arrangement of incident and dialogue, and the relations of the characters, have invariably a close connection with reality. He frequently chucks plausibility completely. He does so in this little play *Over-ruled*. The movement of the characters in dialogue is as symmetrical as figures in a square dance, but the actors had no idea that they were playing highly artificial comedy, with the result that the situations appeared forced, without being funny. The appeal of surface actuality has never had so strong a hold upon the imagination as it has at the present moment (*Broadway* is the acme of this appeal); the influence of the cinema is potent in this direction. Unless people remember that there are dramatic conventions, more suitable to plays addressed to the understanding, not only the plays of Bernard Shaw, but half the repertory of Europe will become unplayable, partly because the actors will not know how to act them, which they are already in danger of forgetting, and partly because such works do not produce that immediate impression of actuality which is universally attractive since it at once engages the most languid attention. An artificial comedy such as *Over-ruled* cannot be played by actors whose skill is limited to imitating the behaviour of people in an hotel lounge. Indeed, the more realistic and unemphatic such mimicry, the more it inevitably swears with the words the actors have to speak. They must know how to put form and flourish into their acting. But there is another ingredient in *Over-ruled* which makes it difficult to play, and it is at this point in my comments, suggested by the complete failure of the Everyman performance, that these preliminary remarks about the gaiety of Mr Shaw become relevant to dramatic criticism. In many of Shaw's plays that temperamental gaiety is pervasive; in all it is apt to make abrupt demands upon his interpreters. *Over-ruled* is a comedy of flirtation in which two men make love to each other's wives, and all four are unexpectedly and, needless to add, artificially confronted. The point of the scene is that all four find their legitimate affections much stronger than their romantic infatuations and that the situation contrasts two types of philanderers: the man who does not care what people do as long as they admit they are doing wrong, and the type who never makes love unless he thinks it is right. 'Love like the intellect grows bright gazing on many truths' would be a sentiment with which the latter would be in agreement, though in practice he is equally certain that it is apt to jeopardise the happiness of others. The contrast between the man of the world moralist and the Shelleyian lover I found extremely amusing and pointful when I read the play. Alas, because the actor was unable to depict fantastic joy, taking the form of intellectual high spirits in the middle of an embrace, the exhilaration of the situation entirely evaporated in performance.

Nowhere in Mr Shaw's plays does this 'irrational gaiety', lending a character sudden fluency and emphasis of speech, require more delicate and ardent interpretation than in his love scenes. Those sudden towerings of the spirit, those blind whiffs of exhilarating joy (the speeches of Valentine the dentist, of the poet in *Candida*, etc.), are even more difficult to act than the flights of combative ecstasy and argumentative indignation so common, yet so seldom perfectly delivered, in his plays. To act gaiety without being clumsy is a rare accomplishment on the stage. Charles Wyndham could achieve it; I remember Granville Barker succeeding as Tanner and as Valentine, thanks to his sympathy with the temperamental quality of their declamations.

The reason I have expatiated on *Over-ruled* is that my colleagues have either completely ignored it or just directed a destructive sniff at it. The reputation of Bernard Shaw is now entering upon that stage in which his originality, after being the private property of the advanced, is becoming common property. In a select audience it is no longer sufficient that a line of his is clearly intended to be funny for it to bring down the house. This is the period in the natural history of reputations in which not only useful sifting is done, but real merits are apt to be ignored. My object in writing this week has been to counteract in some measure any undue encouragement to unbalanced depreciation which may have resulted from the performance of *Over-ruled*.

THE APPLE CART

AND MR BELLOC'S APPLES

September 28, 1929

HE IS, WHAT in youth he never dreamt of becoming, one
of the most popular men in England—I am speaking
of Bernard Shaw. This is not a suspicious symptom,
it is merely the result of having been before the public a long
time. The English have a habit of proclaiming someone as the
Grand Old Man of Letters and of then hailing all he does
afterwards as more wonderful than anything he did before.

'How can I hope to put in a column and a half', wrote Mr St
John Ervine of *The Apple Cart*, 'a fair measure of the brains
that are in it? To produce such a piece of high farce, fantastic
wisdom, high discourse, at the age of seventy-three, is a feat
of which men half the age of Mr Shaw might be envious.'
(Yes, of course, they ought to be.) 'Let me say', wrote another
critic, 'this is one of the most brilliant plays Bernard Shaw has
written. . . .' 'To-day', exclaimed Mr Hannen Swaffer, after
the first performance, 'was a great event in the history of the
English theatre.' Such praise might pass as only verbally careless if critics showed that they also remembered that Mr Shaw
has written many other plays not only as brilliant but more
profound—plays which they received in a very different manner.
What was it, I asked myself, at the end of the performance of
The Apple Cart, beside the dramatist's venerable years, which
made people who were wont to dismiss his 'discussion plays' as
all talk and no drama, accept this prolonged conversation with
such grateful enthusiasm? Not even in *Getting Married* or in
Misalliance is the proportion of talk to action greater than it is
in *The Apple Cart*.

Well, in the first place there is the theatrical reason: with the exception of the interlude, the talk centres upon a situation in which one man is pitted against many, and this is always a 'sympathetic' situation. How is King Magnus going to escape signing the ultimatum by which his Cabinet intends to reduce him to a royal cipher? We are aware that he is cleverer and more disinterested than his ministers, but we are kept wondering how he will manage to get the better of them. He triumphs in the end by threatening to abdicate and lead a rival political party in the House of Commons. Why that threat should have compelled the Prime Minister to tear up the ultimatum was not quite clear to me. Such a decision on his part would depend, of course, upon his estimate of the feeling in the country at the moment, and indications of that were insufficient to make one certain that the Prime Minister's decision was inevitable. One thing, however, was certain, that the King as a party leader would have aimed at destroying the power of the great 'Breakages Trust', allied as it was with a more or less corrupt press; while his own views suggested that to do this he has willingly become a Mussolini under the nominal monarchy of his son. At the same time his last words to Lysistrata (Power Mistress General) hint that he felt himself too old and tired to see that job through. She, who alone in the Cabinet represents devotion to efficiency, was sincerely sorry that he did not abdicate. The implication, then, is that the Labour Cabinet and its Prime Minister are content, now the whole population is enjoying a more or less American level of prosperity, to let the 'Breakages Trust' and corruption alone, provided they remain in office themselves. This is the only assumption on which the effect of the King's threat became plausible.

It is not very long ago since Mr Shaw startled Liberals and reformers by speaking up for Mussolini; and so inveterate is the popular notion that his *obiter dicta* are dictated by desire to surprise that his defence of Fascism was interpreted as a piece of characteristic showy wilfulness. *The Apple Cart* proves it was nothing of the kind. And here we touch upon a second reason why the play has been received with such effusive benevolence. The central idea that emerges from the criss-cross of discussion, from the satire, the fun and the clash of character, is that Democracy as a form of Government is a hopeless fraud. This is a widespread and spreading opinion. The strength of King Magnus's position is that he knows it; and being a King he can afford to admit it, while his Ministers and opponents know it is true, but have to pretend that it is not. It gives him a great pull in argument. The discussion was consequently a one-man walk-over affair between a clever, calm, disinterested man and a set of excitable political boobies, each with one eye askew on the main chance. As a dramatic critic I missed in it therefore what has hitherto been the great merit of Mr Shaw's discussion plays, an even distribution of brains among the debaters.

I have watched for years the evolution of Mr Shaw's thought and genius. We all remember the moment when as a reformer he seemed to despair (if one so instinctively gay in temper can ever be said to do so) and turned to the idea of selective breeding (*Man and Superman*). Later, he found it necessary to add another postulate to the basis of rational optimism; the idea (*Methuselah*) that the world could not really improve until men had learnt how to live to be thousands of years old. Both plays were full of insight into the radical condition of humanity. *The Apple Cart* is nothing of that kind. It is almost as topical as *John Bull's Other Island*, though the scene is projected into the future. That is another reason why it has interested people; it is about things they talk and laugh about. Let us not, then, call *The Apple Cart* 'profound'—brilliantly topical is the right description. Its circumstances only differ from those of to-day in two respects: the national income is at the date of the play so distributed that there is no effective discontent left in England, and life is still more Americanised. But the main features of the political situation remain those of to-day. There is a King who, though glamour has deserted him, still possesses dormant legal powers, by using which an exceptional man might any day make the Throne of first importance in the state. (Magnus is such a king.) Intelligent citizens have lost all interest in politics; the predatory have found short private cuts to power and riches outside politics, though they exert pressure if necessary on frightened politicians through the press, which is in their pockets; the masses give without thinking their votes to any type of man or woman who amuses them; they are better off than they have ever been before, and they don't and *can't* bother their heads about the really precarious nature of that prosperity; they don't know and they don't care how the rich batten on the waste generated by the social machine; politics only attract second-raters who cannot carve out for themselves a career in other fields; the devices by which politicians become popular and 'rise' (but no longer to honour) are so futile as to fill any self-respecting man with nausea; the party machine makes the Cabinet independent of the House of Commons, and Cabinets are full of duds or representatives of dubious 'interests'; the Prime Minister has to use all his wits in trimming between those interests and cajoling those duds, instead of applying them to real problems. But one barrier against corrupt or stupid legislation remains—the Royal Veto; that is to say, the disinterested effective decisions of a man independent of the votes of idiots who are pulled and pushed this way and that by a few energetic, greedy persons, good fellows no doubt in private life, but without the tradition of public service or any understanding of statesmanship. Such is the theme of *The Apple Cart*.

Allowing for exaggerations, all this will pass as a description of English politics to-day. But who was it who drew our attention to these features in the political scene? It was not Mr Shaw. I looked at my programme to make quite sure that *The Apple Cart* had not been written in collaboration with Mr Belloc. Its points were precisely those at which Mr Belloc has been hammering for twenty years: the humbug of modern representative government; the unreality of party conflicts; the poor quality of the men attracted to public life; the helplessness of politicians in the hands of financiers and newspaper proprietors (Mr Belloc wrote with Cecil Chesterton before the war a book on the danger of Press-Combines); the resulting indifference of the public to politics; the dwindling prestige of the House of Commons; the permeation of public life by indirect corruption; the Americanisation and plutocratising of old England. A few years ago, Mr Belloc wrote also a book suggesting the same remedy as *The Apple Cart*—a real King.

When critics of *Major Barbara* were chattering about Mr Shaw's debt to Nietzsche, he pointed at once to Samuel Butler who also was a literary Ishmael. I think he ought to dedicate this play to Mr Belloc. Of course, no reproach is intended in pointing out this rather odd accord between men who have hitherto always met to dispute, but I do object to others who have for years ignored Mr Belloc's criticism of political life as the notions of a somewhat bitter and irresponsible crank, hailing now the same criticisms from Mr Shaw as proofs of startling and original insight. For my part, though agreeing with reservations to both writers' general diagnosis, I seem to hear a small still voice which whispers 'Fiddlesticks', when they proceed to recommend the Royal Veto as a remedy.

The skill is great with which the discussions are supported throughout the play by interest being directed upon the King. The types are amusing, and though caricatures they are recognisably true. King Magnus, unpretentious, subtle and selfless, is not only a real human being, but a creation of Mr Shaw's moral insight, which is a much more remarkable gift than his faculty for hitting off types. It is that gift which makes him the superb dramatist he is. Greatness of mind is not necessarily imposing or magnetic; it is something which may only gradually draw you—such are the virtues of King Magnus. A disinterested man of strong intellect, and without *amour propre*, will often make others round him seem like children. This is the effect of Magnus. At rare moments, when his ministers catch the infection of his candour, they dimly know themselves to be, comparatively speaking, babies. Mr Cedric Hardwicke acted the part with an inconspicuous perfection: no emphasis; transparent moderation in the expression of emotion; absence of obvious charm of manner, except for that quiet charm which springs from respect for the self-respect of others, and, easily overlooked by the stupid, often makes the most fascinating manners look a little vulgar and blatant beside it. Of all the characters in the play, Proteus, the Prime Minister, is the only one, male or female, who is even remotely capable of taking the measure of the King's diameter. Proteus is a clever study. (I thought I recognised in him a hint or two taken from real life.) He is very intelligent; but, alas! the political game has caught him and forced him to devote his faculties to steering adroitly from moment to moment rather than to seeking a goal. Just as Napoleon learnt to use his natural bad temper diplomatically, so does Proteus employ his endowment in the direction of touchy vanity and emotional hysteria to gain time or darken counsel. He is blunt of speech and devious in thought; Magnus is subtle and frank, Proteus crude and uncandid. I admired Mr Charles Carson's impersonation, especially in that it suggested that what poor Proteus needed was time, time—*time* to consider things; while he was always being forced to speak as though he had thought out everything carefully. There was sometimes a wandering glare in his handsome eyes, as of a man trying to remember three things at once; this glare, combined with a worn platform pomposity of speech suited the part exactly.

The interlude is a deft piece of real construction. Apparently it has nothing to do with the theme, yet it supplies what is wanted—a background. Firstly, a background, in the sense of the King's private life, in which he remains exactly the same man; secondly, it reminds us of the *beau monde*, which has turned away from social questions as drab and petty. Magnus, for the sake of a little rest, often visits this world, represented by his putative mistress, Orinthia; wondering, just a little fascinated, at the blooming, gaseous extravagance of its romantic egotism. Orinthia is a more corporeal embodiment of the spirit which animated in *Methuselah* the figures of Ozymandias and Cleopatra-Semiramis, who, you remember, die in that play of 'discouragement' when brought into the presence of moral beauty and endeavour. Orinthia is not subject to such a test. She is quite unaware of Magnus, except that, since he *is* a King, he ought to cut a shining figure on the throne with her beside him. Miss Edith Evans was self-sacrificingly blatant. I think Mr Shaw went a little too far in showing up Orinthia, for it became difficult to believe that Magnus could like her. The feminine foil to her is Queen Jemima, a domestic lady, perfectly dignified in what Orinthia would consider a very dull, humdrum way. Was it quite right, *dramatically*, that Queen Jemima should have been so much more attractive? No.

The richest moment of comedy in the play is when the American ambassador, setting a seal upon what is a *fait accompli*, suggests, radiant with generosity, that America should return again to the British Empire—a proposal which is equivalent to the python saying to a swallowed rabbit 'at last we are one'.

Of course, *The Apple Cart* has rare merits; that anyone should think less of it, or admire it less than they do, is not my object in writing this article. It is to protest against the play being put in the forefront of Mr Shaw's achievements.

TOO TRUE TO BE GOOD

August 13, 1932

TOO TRUE TO BE GOOD is, I take it, one of those titles (*As you Like It* is probably another) which hint at the author's attitude towards the work in question. It has no discernible relation to the play itself, unless—the thought has just crossed my mind—Mr Shaw intended to suggest by his title that his play was mainly about people who were too truthful to believe in current religion or to go on trying to be good. One of the subjects expounded is the predicament of those who have lost faith in any rule of life, and this may have been uppermost in his mind when he named his play. But I like to think that he was also aware that he had been so much more interested in the truths which from time to time he made his characters utter or illustrate, that he had been indifferent about the goodness of this play as a play. It had become in his hands 'too true to be good'. He has certainly never yet shown more complete indifference to form. For form he has never had much heed, and that is one of the main contrasts between him and Ibsen, his great predecessor among 'prophetic' dramatists. Form is not a rigid thing, it is Protean, dependent on the nature of that which the artist intends to convey, but Ibsen always took immense pains to write a story which was capable of being saturated from beginning to end with his theme or themes— sometimes he had several. To achieve this is the triumph of the dramatist's art; it is one of the most difficult things to do, and so it is to create figures for the stage who shall be credible, complex and complete, and yet illustrate typical behaviour in given circumstances—convey an idea, as it is loosely called. Mr Shaw has achieved this in the past. In some of his early plays, such as *Candida*, or in his middle period in such plays as *Man and Superman, Major Barbara, Blanco Posnet, Androcles and the Lion*, there is little waste material, little put in for its own sake which is not absorbed into the theme. But he has always thought art a childish pre-occupation compared with philosophy, and so there has been no check upon his shirking the difficulties of his craft: 'A convincing, interesting story? Are we in the nursery, that we still require to be told a tale? Real people? Are we so stupid as not to know that *all* creation of character is in the end bounce and legerdemain? I can get across with far less effort what I want to say if I let the story go hang, while the more fantastic and improbable my thread of events is the more people will attend to what I want to teach'—some such argument with himself accounts best for the general lines of Bernard Shaw's development as a playwright. In earlier times he was possessed as a dramatist with an impulse to fly from the matter-of-fact. Fact and story hampered him; he could not be bothered with them; he wanted to hurl ideas into our heads. He did, and our heads were the clearer for them. He never could believe that anyone worth addressing cared for economy in the adjustment of means to ends, or for a compact, tightly knit whole. Did a Gaiety Theatre audience bother their heads about meeting again the comic page-boy and all the pretty chamber-maids and peccant husbands of the Imperial Hotel in Act II at Monte Carlo, as long as the fun and songs were to their taste? Of course not. Nor would his 'pit of philosophers' care a rap about his legend or construction provided his ideas were stimulating. (The construction of *Man and Superman* resembles that of a musical comedy). Thus he seems to have argued, and his marvellously apt sense of stage effect, his judgment in timing a joke or extravagant incident to relieve intellectual tension at just the right moment, his passionate sincerity, carried him again and again triumphantly through. But for all this his theory of dramatic art was wrong: it overlooked the fact that the function of art is to *embody* ideas so that they become lastingly memorable, and affect men without their even defining them. It is not its function to provide a series of entertaining excuses for expressing a criticism of life. The latter aim is worth attaining when it is done by a man like Bernard Shaw, but it is not the thing *most* worth doing by a dramatist.

Here is a small proof of it. Here am I, an attentive playgoer, yet I can't tell you what the play I have just seen at the Malvern Festival is about. I could have told you what *Major Barbara* was about; I could have told you what *Getting Married* was about, because, though there was no story in which the theme was embodied, the characters at any rate discussed one theme— marriage; and their various slants upon that problem were most illuminating. But in *Too True to be Good* there are dozens of subjects. I have forgotten nine-tenths of the best things, because there was no focus to group them round. As I sat in the stalls I kept exclaiming to myself, 'Ah, that goes deep; that's worth thinking about'. But afterwards I did not know what general conclusion I, or rather Mr Shaw, had reached. The play seemed to me a series of snapshots taken from different angles of a post-war state of mind. But it was not a picture of that state of mind. The play did not embody it. It was more like a series of notes of all the things that playwright would somehow have to work in if his picture of that state of mind were to be anything like complete.

I can, however, report what Mr Shaw intended the play to be about, because while we critics were being carried, as the guests of Sir Barry Jackson, to the scene of action in a sumptuous aeroplane, a printed letter from Mr Shaw was distributed among us.

Now I have criticised his plays again and again, and in doing so I have always obtained valuable clues from his own criticism of them. Sometimes his prefaces have enabled me to see defects I should not otherwise have noticed. 'The moral of my play', he wrote in this printed letter, 'or rather the position illustrated by it, is simple enough.' (I must condense). The last war differed from all others in bringing home to people that war means slaughter and barbarity. 'When terror had gone to its limit, subsequent indulgence for everything, from the pitch and toss of a night at *The Byng Boys* to the manslaughter of a correspondent, obeyed the law that action and reaction are equal. And so, for four years, it was taken as a matter of course that young people, when they were not under fire, must be allowed a good time.

'Now I do not at all object to young people having a good time. I think they should have a good time all the time, at peace as well as in war. I think that their having a good time is one of the tests of civilisation. But I very strenuously warn both young and old against the monstrous folly of supposing that a good time has any resemblance to those wartime reactions after paroxysms of horror and terror, when the most childish indulgence seemed heavenly and the most reckless excesses excusable on the plea of 'Let us eat and drink (especially drink); for to-morrow we die.' Our difficulty now is that what the bright young things after the war tried to do, and what their wretched survivors are still trying to do, is to get the reaction without the terror, to go on eating cocaine and drinking cocktails as if they had only a few hours' expectation of life instead of forty years.

'In my play the ex-war nurse and the ex-airman ace persuade a respectable young lady—too respectable to have ever had a good time—to come with them and enjoy the sort of good time they had in the nightmare of 1914-18. My stage picture of the result of the experiment will, I hope, deter any respectable young lady who witnesses it from relieving the tedium and worthlessness of idle gentility in that way.'

But, Mr Shaw, it won't and can't, your play, do anything of the kind. You have not drawn a picture of a post-war 'good time'. All you have shown to respectable young ladies is one of their class getting so well and strong among the mountains that her own mother does not recognise her and adopts her. You have made her fall passionately in love with a burglar who enters her bedroom in the first act, and elope with him to wild places, and then declare, 'Strange as it may seem, our relations are perfectly innocent.' What are you thinking of? Where is the analogy in all this to the nightmare dissipation you want to warn the young against? True, you make her exclaim, 'I'm free and well, but I'm bored because I have no aim in life', but any pre-war young woman might say that at moments. Where is your theme? And, apropos of your theme, what is the connection between it and the first act? The first act is farcical Christian Science; it suggests that the proper way to cure measles is to jump out of bed, put on your clothes, and run into the night. Granted that is true, which it is not, what has it to do with post-war mentality? And what warning is there in the spectacle of the ex-nurse who, having always acted on the supposition that the first ten days of an affair were the pleasantest, and continually changed her lovers, has kept her self-respect intact, and when 'Mr Right' comes along, in the shape of a Bunyan-Bible-reading sergeant, settles down into a steady wife? Evidently, Mr Shaw is not thinking about his theme, nor what he intended to write about. Fortunately, I only glanced at his account of his aims before I had seen the play itself, so I was able to enjoy it thoroughly as a miscellany of illuminating comments upon war, peace,. sex, and religion, distributed among puppets who were amusing without being real, and in nearly all cases admirably interpreted. The elocution of Mr Cedric Hardwicke was admirable; he had not much acting to do. The passionate speech of the religious atheist who finds himself in an undetermined Universe with all the old certainties obliterated, was well worth listening to, and spoken with excellent intensity by Mr Ayliff, haranguing us like an old St. Jerome from his cave. The finish of the impossible nurse's performance (Miss Ellen Pollock) was admirable; she had opportunities for acting and took them. The nurse is the mouthpiece of observations spoken from 'the lower centres of man', and many of these are memorable and pointful, so also are the comments of the Bible-loving sergeant on war, religion, and the City of Destruction. The final speech, that of the Burglar (Mr Cedric Hardwicke) was an astonishing and moving feat.

GENEVA

A PLAY OF THE MOMENT

December 3, 1938

I F YOU DO not find *Geneva* amusing that will probably be due either to the lack of sympathy in yourself for Hitler, Franco and Mussolini, or to some of the jokes in it being too often repeated. They are not all bad jokes, some are very good indeed, but it is also true that there are an unusual number of what Mr Shaw once called 'thistles for donkeys' in the dialogue, and that the fun of the intellectual knock-about does not always excite the hilarity it loudly demands.

Some of the figures (in an extravaganza 'characters' would be out of place) are boring—notably two females. One is called Begonia Brown and the other 'A Widow', who is dressed in the black lace mantilla of a Spanish woman and carries a revolver in her vanity bag. Miss Alison Leggatt's intonations, gestures, accent, as Begonia, left nothing to be desired; and Miss Phillippa Gill put a wonderfully undiminished energy into even the third repetition of the same burlesquely melodramatic turn which fell to her lot. But it was in vain. The exaggerated self-assurance of Begonia of Camberwell becomes monotonous, and we listen to the Widow's tirades with the blankness of those who cannot guess what they are meant to feel. Is it amusement, pity or moral condemnation! It is possible, I know, to feel all three towards the same object; but to enable us to do so that object must be presented with much more subtlety than in the part which Miss Gill performs with such good will. All the interpreters of this puppet-show deserve high praise; and if one cannot help distinguishing the glorious performances of Mr Ernest Thesiger as Sir Orpheus Midlander, the British Foreign Secretary (he looks extraordinarily like Sir Austen Chamberlain), and of Mr Cecil

Trouncer as Bombardoni, it is because those are far the best parts. They were given something worth making the most of, and they did. But Mr William Heilbronn as A Newcomer (the representative modern democrat), Mr Knox as The Judge, Mr Walter Hudd as Battler, dressed in the shining armour of Siegfried, Mr Stuart Lindsay as General Flanco de Fortinbras, the nervous Bishop (Mr Hignett), the distributor of Come-to-Jesus tracts (Miss Milbourne), and the rest, all struck me as being what they were meant to be. The feeble impression made by Mr Donald Eccles was the fault of the part, not the actor. In this disputatious extravaganza, which Mr Shaw calls 'A Play of the Moment', the case for the Jew ought of course to have been vigorously put. It was not. Nor was the case of the democrat who was represented as a red-faced, heavy-paunched, muddle-headed gaby. When The Newcomer complains before the Court of International Justice that the leader of a party standing for a 'Business Democracy' has turned the opposition out of Parliament with an army of 'Clean Shirts', and destroyed freedom of speech and democracy in the country, Bombardoni retorts, 'How can you destroy what never existed? What I give fools like you is good government, and if you kick against it I put you in concentration camps.' Mr Shaw leaves it at that. Surely a little one-sided? The case of the Jew against Battler is most deplorably handled. 'I have been robbed and beaten', he cries. 'I am sorry', Battler retorts, 'I cannot be everywhere and all my agents are not angels.' If Mr Shaw could not remember an answer to that he should not have attempted 'A Play of the Moment'. If he did, and withheld it, he has been false to his mission in life. Until recent years one of the things I have admired most in him has been a spontaneous chivalry; an impulse to stick up for the helpless, and never to abet those who kick them when they were down. When a false astronomical rumour that the end of the world is at hand breaks up the Court at the Hague Bombardoni says he will die at his post; Battler sheds tears at the thought that his dog must perish:

'My doggie, my poor little doggie' (I do not see the point of this); Sir Orpheus implores everyone to contradict the rumour at once, so that chaos may not set in a day earlier than is inevitable (I do see the point of that as a revelation of the English method of handling crises); Flanco with complete equanimity leaves the matter to the Catholic Church; Begonia refuses a 'choc'; the female evangelist weeps because she has been so happy bringing sins and sorrows to Jesus, while in Heaven there will not be any to bring—and the Jew? He bolts for the telephone to sell his gilt-edge securities in order that he may buy them back at the price of waste paper, thus dying, at any rate nominally, a millionaire. What do you think of introducing such an incident, *and at this moment in European History*, as symbolic of the soul of the Jewish race when revealed under the stress of disaster? Speaking for myself, it made me ask if it were possible that I had been a fool about Bernard Shaw all my writing life. I don't think I have. But in order to explain the difference between the G.B.S. of the past and of recent years, I have now, as a critic, to be what may seem cruel and offensive. Yet it is the only way of suggesting an explanation of a change in the man who wrote, say, the Preface for Politicians (*John Bull's Other Island*) with its indictment of those who hanged and flogged some wretched Arabs for having mobbed some British pigeon-shooters at Denshawai; who wrote of that 'horror' as he called it, in a spirit worthy of the last words of one of those Arabs on the scaffold, 'May God compensate us well for this world of meanness, for this world of injustice, for this world of cruelty'; a man who wrote again and again, as a publicist and as a dramatist, words which awoke in others the feeling that in a world without justice or mercy it was man's duty to put them there.

What has happened to him? He has grown old, and in his old age he has watched the most merciless of all revolutions achieving in Russia what, theoretically, was a fulfilment of a political system he approved.

The first process, common to us all, has blunted his human sympathies; the second has forced him logically into an inhuman leniency towards similar methods in other Totalitarian States. If you read his Preface to *On the Rocks* (1933), you will find a defence of 'liquidation' of all persons who resist the policy of a Government. You will hear echoes of that view in the summing up of the Judge in *Geneva*.

Now, what *is* this process of growing old, which all past middle age can watch in themselves, and once prompted Shaw to write in the *Revolutionist's Hand Book*, with pardonable and amusing exaggeration, 'Every man over forty is a scoundrel'. In human beings as a rule the heart, the power to feel, withers before the head. Our faculties, our aptitudes, if we have any, may remain unimpaired. You can see this process clearest in the final stages of senility. A very old person when told that their nearest and dearest have been killed, bursts into tears and the next moment says, 'Why can't you remember that I don't like marmalade for tea.' The emotion at the moment may be intense, but the power of sustaining it gets weaker and weaker. The snare of old age is mistaking indifference for wisdom. That is why the young discount so heavily and properly the advice of the old; the old have forgotten what they are talking *about*. When Mr Shaw began to be conscious of this inevitable tendency in himself, instead of being on guard against it, he wrote *Methuselah*, in which complete detachment from the passions was glorified, as the one qualification for controlling the world. Incidentally, this relaxation of the power of holding an emotion is the mark of works produced in old age. The workmanship in detail may remain brilliant, but the work as a whole will lack coherence, for in creative work it is emotion that guides the intellect. The books of the old are apt to be ramshackle, garrulous and repetitive; being unable to sustain emotion they are apt to lose their way in their own works. They may reach conclusions in the course of them, but they cannot create a coherent whole. This has been painfully obvious in the recent plays of Mr Shaw, while his recent comments on the state of the world have been marked by a chirpy indifference to realities. He has been unable to write a page which did not betray his secret, that he can no longer feel anything much.

The limitations of his drama have been due to a weakness in portraying human emotions from within, with the exception of one passion, the grandest of all, namely, the passion of a man to whom success in life means the identification of himself with a cause greater than himself. But he has, like an artist, often used this disability to produce most original comedy, and it has been compensated by an exceptional fairness which has enabled him to lend his own remarkable intellect to his dramatic protagonists. What impresses us in so many of his old plays is the hammer-and-tongs vigour and brilliance with which each combatant stands up for his side. As I have indicated, in *Geneva* this distribution is far from impartial. No doubt Mr Shaw intended the summing up of the Judge to correct any bias. But dramatically it does nothing of the kind. For the Judge's sentence condemns everybody equally, which is equivalent to a general acquittal, and by no means redresses the feebleness with which the case *against* Bombardoni, Battler and Flanco has been put. Even the moral 'that man is a failure as a political animal' and therefore doomed to self-destruction, is not felt with the energy of Swift or Voltaire. The irrational fountain of gaiety continues to play. The close is a bland dismissal of the vital issues which have been at stake in the debate. 'Do not blaspheme', said Flanco, and he has all our sympathy, 'at such a moment by telling us that nothing matters'. And even that verdict on man in his political capacity is not resolute. The curtain falls on the Judge saying, 'It has not been a farce. Then *came* those fellows,' meaning the Dictators, 'they blustered and defied us. But they came.' He might have added, 'And had the best of the argument, which is what will impress the public.'

THE DEVIL'S DISCIPLE

August 3, 1940

BERNARD SHAW'S *The Devil's Disciple* is on at the Piccadilly
Theatre. Excellent drama it is, though the performance
leaves much to be desired. Mr Robert Donat plays the
part of Dick Dudgeon, who gives his nickname to the piece,
and Mr Donat's robust, vital, handsome presence and trenchant
manner of speech fit him to play a stout-hearted hero in
Melodrama. For that is what *The Devil's Disciple* is. It is
old-fashioned Melodrama only with a difference; that difference
being that the dramatist had something new to say in 1897 which
he was burning to express about 'heroism' and the way that
on the stage it had been hitherto invariably linked with 'love'
as its motive. This inevitable association had disgusted both
the puritan mystic and the realistic observer of human nature
in Shaw. And, Heavens! how that association had bored
(often to *our* great entertainment) the dramatic critic of *The
Saturday Review*, G.B.S. It had not escaped his notice that
among the instances of one person either risking or giving his
life for another recorded in the papers, as often as not there had
not been even acquaintance between them. And 'when we
want to read of the deeds that are done for love', he added in
the Preface to *Plays for Puritans*, 'whither do we turn? To the
murder column; and there we are rarely disappointed'. There is
exaggeration, over-simplification here, for there is love and
love; but what an exhilarating change it was to hear Dick (it
was at Kennington Theatre in 1898 that I first heard him)
gently but firmly disabusing Judith Anderson of the notion
that love for her had prompted his sudden impulse to take her
husband's place on the scaffold; a denial all the more piquant
because the grave, pretty, romantic young wife had, at the time,
more than half a mind to him herself, in spite of her devotion

to her elderly clerical husband and of Dick's horrifying but rather thrilling impiety. The contrast between the self-sacrifice of a courageous ruffian and the alacrity with which her husband had, apparently, taken advantage of it proved too much for Judith, until, by saving both Dick's neck and his own, he re-established himself in her heart.

As Shaw pointed out himself, the play contained the stock ingredients which were the delight of old Adelphi audiences: the scapegrace with a better nature who protects an oppressed orphan, the reading of a will in his favour, the heroic sacrifice, the court-martial, scaffold and reprieve. This did not prevent him from being praised and abused for reckless originality. The critics fixed upon what they supposed to be subversive in the play, taking Dick for a blackguard and Mrs. Dudgeon for a religious woman. Regarding Dick's loyalty to the Devil, Shaw—who had been much amused by the play's reception—wrote: 'Let those who have praised my originality read Blake's *Marriage of Heaven and Hell*; and I shall be fortunate if they do not rail at me for a plagiarist.' But there, I think, his diagnosis is at fault.

The devil whom Dick worshipped was, like Blake's, a redeemer who preached a gospel of energy; to whom both malignant fears that lead to cruelty and timid fears that create hypocrisy were The Enemy. But there the resemblance ends. The evangel of the identity of body and soul, with its corollary that desire is sacred and an *end in itself*, and abstinence distortion, had no place in the Puritan rebelliousness of Shaw's *Devil's Disciple*. For the first time, the Religion of Progress peeps out in Shaw's drama, when Dick, the rope about his neck and speaking what he believes will be his last words, shouts: 'Amen! my life for the world's future.' Later in Shaw's development this was to become explicit as the doctrine of the Life-Force.

Although every dramatist is usually the better for having 'a message', that is to say something to say which he believes to be of the utmost urgency, his work may lose something by his becoming more and more conscious of its nature. His sense of its importance may then lead him to prefer to express it explicitly through the mouths of one or two characters, rather than to embody it in situations. With a few exceptions (*Saint Joan* and *Blanco Posnet*, for example) in the plays which followed *Major Barbara*, what is said on the stage is of clearly more interest to the dramatist than what happens. Unlike Ibsen, the later Shaw troubled little about construction. Provided he could think of an excuse, however thin, for making his figures talk about what he wanted discussed he was satisfied. He cared less and less about exhibiting emotion or character in action, especially in cumulative action, which is the essence of drama. He fell back more and more often on haphazard incidents of farce (somebody knocking somebody else down—usually a woman flooring a man) to satisfy that legitimate desire to see something happen which exists in every audience.

Although *The Devil's Disciple* is a bag of old tricks, they are used to drive home a deeper emotion and a moral contrary to the ethics of melodrama. Not only does the hero of this one disappoint the expectations excited by his romantic role by repudiating the notion that he was sacrificing his life for the heroine's sake; but this heroism itself is finally exhibited to a disadvantage beside the really efficient though unself-sacrificing energy of a robust, entirely prosaic parson. There lay the really surprising originality of this play; in this sudden reversal of the relative positions of the hero and the husband at the end. Everything that had happened before had made us feel the superiority of Dick; but however keenly we had felt that, or the dramatist himself had sympathised with him, he was not going to permit us to exalt martyrdom above effective service in a cause. He makes Dick, as he steps down from the gallows (enormously relieved, though with a slightly rueful sense of anti-climax), say to Anderson: 'If I had been any good, I should have done for you what you did for me (i.e., ride for help to the approaching American forces) instead of making a vain sacrifice.' 'Not vain, my boy', is the reply. 'It takes all sorts to make a world—saints as well as soldiers.' And the ex-Presbyterian minister, now a soldier, 'has it', as they say in carrying resolutions at meetings.

Act II, which leads up to this deposition of the hero who offers his life to save another, is as good an act as Shaw ever wrote. It is not as deeply interesting as some others, but (to apply the Anderson test) it is as efficient as the best in achieving what it set out to do. It contains three striking emotional shifts-over; the character contrasts are tightly interwoven with action; masculine and feminine points of view are well juxtaposed, and the curtain falls on *our* knowledge that Judith Anderson does not understand her husband—a good climax.

But, alas, this production makes but a poor job of it, chiefly owing to a gross miscasting in the part of Anthony Anderson. From the opening of the play the indications are clear that the minister of this small New Hampshire community during the war of American Independence is a man of exceptional force, directness and self-confidence. He thinks Dick a bit of a ruffian; he is not in the least like the others afraid of him, and takes Dick's gibes at his cloth with indifference. He has no illusions about the nature of old Mrs Dudgeon's piety and understands the nature of his pretty young wife's feelings towards Dick (half-repulsion, half-attraction) a great deal better than she does herself. Yet he does not hesitate to leave them together at a call of duty, and with an equanimity that is only disturbed for a few minutes when he finds her on his return lying on the floor in a faint after Dick's arrest. The way he thinks instantly of her before he even attempts to satisfy the torture of his own anxiety about what has happened in his absence, exhibits his intensely practical nature as well as a very firm benevolence. And for this rock of a man who, when he does learn the nature of the situation, roars for his pistols and all the money in the house, brushing aside his wife's questions as he wrenches on his riding boots (there is not a minute to lose if he is to fetch help in time), the producer has cast an actor with a cosy, mild clerical voice and incapable of energetic gestures. As though the important point about Anderson was that he should suggest the parson! One of the emotional pivots of the play is, of course, that after being impressed by the loquacious dramatic hero the audience should have the opportunity of comparing his carriage and behaviour with the, if anything, greater virility of the realistic hero.

In the part of Judith there are more opportunities for acting than Miss Rosamund Toler availed herself of, but she was adequate. Miss Janet Barrow should remember that though the part of Mrs Dudgeon is pitched in a single key, it is for her interpreter to introduce shades into that old woman's grating harshness. Mr Donat, as I hinted, fills his part well—especially in the first two acts. Granted a suitable personality, there is no particular difficulty in the part—until Dick has to stand on the cart beneath the gallows, while at moments the dialogue veers away from him as a central figure. Here the actor must not forget for an instant to simulate the tortured trepidation of a man who is about to have his neck broken, and on the degree to which he succeeds in simulating that, and the courage which controls it, wil llargely depend the effect of General Burgoyne's imperturbable politeness: I felt Mr Donat rather failed us then. Mr Milton Rosmer in the part of 'Gentleman Johnny' clearly enjoyed himself as much as we enjoyed him, which was a good deal. I think I could have stood even more blandness in his irony, and certainly a touch of more peremptory gravity when he reproves the officer in charge for allowing Judith to be present at the execution. The last minute or two of the play are difficult to stage; more attempt should have been made to follow the dramatist's directions.

FANNY'S FIRST PLAY

September 30, 1944

FANNY'S FIRST PLAY was the first of Shaw's to have a really long run. It was produced at the Little Theatre, in April, 1911, and at the Kingsway Theatre afterwards it continued to run for over a year and a half. I cannot understand why he called it 'a pot-boiler'; it belongs to that serious section of his dramatic works, his religious farces. He did not write a preface to it, perhaps because he had already expatiated upon family life, parents and children, in connection with *Misalliance* (1910), while others among his 'conversion' plays were bigger hooks on which to hang his religious views. But the note he did prefix to it bears exclusively upon its theme, unlike most of his prefaces, which were apt to deal with matters not actually dramatised in the plays for which they were written. Shaw's prefaces are, as a rule, stimulating appendices. In this note he goes straight to the point of the play itself:

Nowadays we do not seem to know that there is any other test of conduct except morality; and the result is that the young had better have their souls awakened by disgrace, capture by the police, and a month's hard labour, than drift along from their cradles to their graves doing what other people do for no other reason than that other people do it, and knowing nothing of good and evil, of courage and cowardice, or indeed anything but how to keep hunger and concupiscence and fashionable dressing within the bounds of good taste except when their excesses can be concealed. Is it any wonder that I am driven to offer to young people in our suburbs the desperate advice: Do something that will get you into trouble? . . . I hate to see dead people walking about: it is unnatural. Out of the mouth of Mrs Knox I have delivered on them the judgment of her God.

Yes, that is the theme of *Fanny's First Play*. And it follows that Mrs Knox is the linchpin of it. Failure to recognise that was the gravest defect (there were other minor ones) of the performance at the Arts Theatre. Miss Cecily Hamilton was extraordinarily impressive in that part in the memorable first production, but Miss Chris Castor, alas, does not come within miles of suggesting that she is a woman who has found 'inner happiness', and knows that its attainment matters most to human beings. She did not seem to know what her own part or the play itself was about, and I expect that few who saw it for the first time did so either. None of the remarkable things Mrs Knox has to say told. Miss Castor never spoke with the authority of one capable of a deeper sincerity than those around her. If the producer had looked up Miss Cecily Hamilton's memoirs and seen what Mrs Knox looked like, that at any rate might have helped the actress to avoid being merely a kind, flustered, tearful elderly matron. Quakerish severity in dress, a touch of the Salvation Army in her bonnet, might have helped to remind her of her part; that she is a woman who can say before her husband:

'I wanted a man who had that happiness within himself. You made me think you had it; but it was nothing but being in love with me.'

'And do you blame him for that?'

'I blame nobody. But let him not think he can walk by his own light. I tell him that if he gives up being respectable he'll go right down to the bottom of the hill. He has no powers inside himself to keep him steady; so let him cling to the powers outside him.'

This is the essence, too, of all the fun throughout; of two elderly tradesmen clinging desperately to conventions in circumstances in which their habitual standards afford no guidance; of everybody, even Mrs. Knox herself for a while, being knocked off their perches by the disgrace of a son and a daughter.

Miss Daphne Arthur as Margaret Knox was very properly in a state of excitement from her first entrance onwards; but she did not keep enough energy in reserve for a crescendo, and there are also passages in which she should appear disconcertingly calm rather than obstreperously defiant. In these she was not equally successful.

In the scene with Bobbie Gilbey which ends in one of those rough and tumbles between a man and stronger woman in which Shaw (to me rather incomprehensibly) delights, it is a mistake for the two young people when they are quarrelling to stand rigidly rubbing noses and shout into each others' faces. That is a stupid modern stage convention supposed to be the expression of intensity. As a matter of fact it destroys the illusion of reality.

I missed the prologue and epilogue in which Shaw ridiculed successfully contemporary dramatic critics who run down his plays. I suppose they were thought to date too much to interest an audience to-day. I think the management was wrong; they are amusing and pointful. *Fanny's First Play* was born of three elements: the suffragette movement (women were on the warpath throwing convention and respectability to the winds), Shaw's impulse to answer his critics, and his growing interest in the significance of religious conversions. I have one hint for Mr Bird, who plays the delightful part of the aristocratic footman. There are moments when he should, while preserving, of course, a well-mannered aloofness, relax his professional rigidity.

THE SIMPLETON OF THE UNEXPECTED ISLES

DESPERATE REMEDIES

March 24, 1945

THE SIMPLETON OF THE UNEXPECTED ISLES which the Arts Theatre actors are now performing at The Arts Theatre Club in Great Newport Street, was first acted at Malvern in 1935. There, as some readers will remember, a Shaw Season was held during successive summers, and these performances I occasionally attended as a grumpy old admirer; one by no means disposed to accept his latter-day plays as wonderful from top to bottom. Malvern became for a short time a sort of Bernard Shaw Bayreuth. The audiences struck me as over-enthusiastic over plays clearly inferior to those of his prime, and the atmosphere was too balmy for my taste. Moreover, some of these latter plays were infected with the infernal Fuhrer-prinzip, then so active everywhere abroad. Recall *On the Rocks*, its conclusion and its Preface. The Preface advocated 'killing as a political function'; 'What we are confronted with now', it stated, 'is a growing perception that if we desire a certain type of civilisation and culture we must exterminate the sort of people who do not fit into it.' It recommended 'Liquidation' as the right way of dealing with the 'unsatisfactory'; 'it is only weeding the garden.' An approved example given was that of 'the unfortunate Commissar who as Minister of Transport found himself obliged to put a pistol in his pocket and with his own hand shoot stationmasters who had thrown his telegrams into the dustbin instead of attending to them, so that he might the more impressively ask the rest of the staff whether they yet grasped the fact that orders are meant to be executed.' Note the placing of the adjective 'unfortunate'. Others (among them the children, wives and friends of some incompetent stationmaster) might be more inclined to apply it to the victim himself than his executioner; for life can be precious also to the incompetent, and the incompetent dear to others.

In *On the Rocks* the old democrat who has striven all his life for universal suffrage and found it has not led to the millennium was made to say: 'It took the heart out of old Hipney; and now I'm for any Napoleon, or Mussolini or Lenin or Chavender' (the chief politician in the play) 'that has the stuff in him to take both the people and the spoilers and oppressors by the scruff of their silly necks and just sling them into the way they should go with as many kicks as may be needful to make a thorough job of it.' It was too early (1933) for Hipney to add 'Heil Hitler'. The same doctrine was put into the mouth of Sir Arthur Chavender. He is made to confess that he himself is not ruthless enough to play the part of the saviour of society, adding, 'I shall hate the man who will carry it through for his cruelty and the desolation he will bring to us and our like.'

I am writing in the parlour of a pleasant public-house beside a small fire. Four jolly tars have just come in, their caps pushed back from the healthy, shiny, vacant, handsome faces. They have ordered pints and are presently going into the next room to play pool. A heavy commercial gent on a high stool leans across the bar drowsily reading an evening paper. So, counting the plump, prompt, bored barmaid herself, there are seven of us here; and a glance within and a glance around tells me for certain sure that we ought to be 'liquidated'. From the point of view of establishing a Communist Utopia we are one and all useless. To say we don't care a fig about mankind would be perhaps an exaggeration; but the condition in which men may be living on this globe at some distant date occupies our thoughts and emotions very little and very seldom compared with our personal satisfactions and the happiness of those near to us. Those four sailors are risking, and willingly, their lives for their 'country', though they don't know exactly what they mean by that. They would probably also take risks to rescue anybody who fell into the Thames which I can see flowing past the window. But if you told them to risk themselves in order that a number of unborn beings might some day be better off they would tell you to go to hell. The heroine of another of Shaw's later plays, 'The Patient' in *Too True to be Good*, cries out in the process of her conversion to the Life Force that she and those around her are merely 'walking machines for turning good food into bad manure'. I don't see why she should have said 'bad' manure, but that somewhat Swiftian verdict is applicable also to us in this room, and—hullo!—to this new arrival; though I fancy G.B.S. would be particularly sorry to see him bumped painlessly off. A black and white Dalmatian dog has just come up to me to be patted. Now, if I could discover a cure for cancer by experimenting on him, I know that Shaw would think me unpardonably wicked and cruel, attributing my intentions merely to unconscious sadism; though why that should be more cruelly wicked than to shoot an incompetent stationmaster in order that a state railway might run better in future, I do not understand. 'Yes, spotted animal, judged by any contribution to world-betterment you are likely to make, your existence cannot possibly be excused. You're just a charge upon the community; true, a lighter one than I, still someone has to feed you. And do you live for your puppies' puppies' puppies? I'm afraid not. Come here, I'll scratch you behind the ears and whisper in them a secret: *no more do I*. I've been to see an amusing, rather faulty play called *The Simpleton of the Unexpected Isles*, which the author rightly calls 'a vision of judgment', and we are both for it. Instead of running after bones and bitches, or sitting by the fire—those things are merely doggish, or, to put it frankly, hoggish—you ought to be striving that in the future dogs should have more bitches and bones. No, that isn't quite right. Say, rather, that at long last dogs should be born which do not want such things; though what they'll be wanting instead I'm not clear. Anyhow, you be off now, and talk to one of those sailors. Only for Heaven's sake don't worship him. He's only human like you. Never take your eyes off the Life Force, though you don't see it, in order to take into account a mere man. Tell him I said so and see what he'll say.'

The Simpleton of the Unexpected Isles (farce in form but serious in content) is a bright and ready impromptu product of Shaw's imagination. It is not of much value itself, but it is interesting from the point of his development. It is quite well acted at the Arts Theatre. Indeed, unless by a piece of rare luck the part of the Oriental priestess could be taken by a quite enormously impressive woman (Miss Paget-Bowman as Prola was, by the way, excellent), I doubt whether much more could be made of the play than the present cast actually do. The comic naturalism of such parts as the shanghaied curate, the colonial governor and his wife, the redeemed emigration officer, the pert little female tourist, only required from their interpreters some humour and enough professional intelligence to keep it within bounds, and thus allow the jokes (all are not very good) to make their effect. Pra, the priest, must be calm, dark and handsome; and Mr Dignam was. The less the apocalyptic angel acts, and the more his behaviour resembles that of a guest arriving at a garden-party with interesting news, the more will the audience enjoy his coming out of the sky, his nightgown and white woolly wings, and the fact that this is indeed the Day of Judgment. Tall Mr Shine, with his fair moustache and social composure, met these requirements; just as, previously, Mr Peter Jones, as the Simpleton or Curate, had exhibited just about the right amount of natural embarrassment on finding that he had to marry both the island lovelies, and not only the one he had at first fancied most. Let me explain.

This island, a British possession, is inhabited also by a pair of Oriental sages, man and wife. Like other characters in Shaw's drama who live on a higher plane, they exercise an irresistible sex-attraction over ordinary mortals, and in this case they take advantage of the infatuation they inspire respectively in the male and female British to try a eugenic experiment and blend in their offspring the virtues of East and West. Twenty years pass. Physically, the offspring are all that could be desired. None will wonder that the Curate, deposited by pirates, fell for the two girls. But mentally and spiritually they are far from satisfactory; they have no conscience; that is why the priest and priestess insist on the curate, who is nothing if not scrupulous, mating both, thus introducing a little conscience into the stock, while as a religious man he should learn that sex is an entirely impersonal relation.

On the stage these eugenic failures appear as allegorical figures, as 'the four lovely phantoms, who embody all the artistic, romantic and military ideals of our cultured suburbs'— Love, Pride, Heroism and Empire. No one, however, would guess this without being told. As Mr E. Strauss points out in his *Bernard Shaw: Art and Socialism*, a book I am never tired of recommending, this fantastic play is to all intents a repetition, on an inferior dramatic level, of one of his very best, *Heartbreak House*: 'For quite obviously Mrs Hushabye is Love, Lady Utterwood is Pride, Hector Hushabye is Heroism and Sir Hastings Utterwood is Empire.' But they are living individuals and these mechanical dolls. Moreover, *The Simpleton* also ends apocalyptically, but with its catastrophe treated in a very different spirit. Shaw had recovered his good spirits (perhaps he has again lost them since); the fountain of glorious gaiety in him has begun once more to spout and sparkle. His faith in the Life Force is again serene, in spite of the collapse of previous hopes.

Now, how interesting this is from the point of view of his changes as a creative dramatist! He begins by writing for the stage as a social reformer, as a Fabian showing up particular abuses. Then follow miscellaneous dramas, till in *Major Barbara* the doctrine is preached that the only hope is to convert the Capitalists—the Undershafts and Bodgers.

The artist is still searching for the fundamental remedy. Of being born again and born better we hear no more. Religion becomes more prominent and results in that splendid climax *Saint Joan*. Then another change: in *Back to Methuselah* religion is blent with the theory that the most vital thing is that men should outlive all their passions; and human being centuries old fill the world. Then the war of 1914: for the first time Shaw writes a tragedy, *Heartbreak House*. Lastly, the post-war period beginning with *The Apple Cart*. This now introduces the *Fuhrer-prinzip*. And last of all *The Simpleton*. What now is the surviving basis of his hopes? Painless Annihilation of Unsuitables; for that, not punishment of course, is Shaw's Day of Judgment. It is a remedy which can only be treated in a spirit of comedy, for looked at realistically there are too many objections to it.

A PERSONAL MEMOIR

1950

IN 1902 I began my career as a literary journalist by writing reviews for *The Speaker* and when the dramatic critic Reginald Farrer, whose name is still remembered as a botanist, left England to hunt for flowers in Tibet, the editor, J. L. Le B. Hammond, thought he would try me as a stopgap. My first contribution as a dramatic critic was an account of a performance of *The Taming of the Shrew*. Years afterwards I was dismayed to find that it was quite up to the standard of my later work. With experience I became a far better judge of acting, but as a judge of the possibilities of a play I seemed to have reached as far as it was in me to go in early youth and my prematurity had at least this advantage that *The Speaker* kept me on even after Farrer's return. His heart however was in the world of flowers (it was he, by the by, who brought the Blue Poppy to England) so, although he used to describe me as his hated rival, he had little difficulty in forgiving me.

My great opportunity came when Granville Barker, with Vedrenne as his business manager, took the Court Theatre in October, 1904. That memorable theatrical enterprise lasted until January 29th, 1907. During that time 32 plays by 17 authors were produced and 946 performances were given. The first performance of six matinées of *Candida* in April and May of 1904, one of which is described in this book, are not regarded as belonging strictly to the Vedrenne-Barker series. This series included eleven plays by Shaw covering 701 performances, three by Euripides and two by Ibsen. Among the others were plays by Granville Barker himself (*The Voysey Inheritance* and *Prunella*, the latter written in collaboration with Laurence Housman), Galsworthy (*The Silver Box*), Hauptmann (*The Thieves' Comedy*), and Masefield (*The Camden Wonder*) to mention only the most important.

It was not until after the publication of *Man and Superman* that I made Bernard Shaw's acquaintance. I have always been in temperament a hero-worshipper, though not on paper, where a more detached being took the pen, and in my youth I tried to meet as many of those writers whom I admired as I could. G. M. Trevelyan had taken me down to see Meredith. I had found Henry James and Hardy on my own initiative. Harley Granville Barker promised to take me to see Shaw if I would take him to see Meredith and sure enough in 1906 we went together to lunch with Mr and Mrs Shaw, who were then living in a flat in Adelphi Terrace. I remember feeling a little embarrassed because I had written a long and in places caustic article on *Man and Superman* in *The Independent Review* and, with that tendency which a young man has of exaggerating the impression that he is likely to make, I supposed that I might have wounded the eminent dramatist and thinker. I was only to discover afterwards that Shaw found it perfectly easy to forgive and ignore the comments of critics.

Two impressions of that visit have remained with me. Harley must have said that he and I were going to visit Meredith for I remember saying to Shaw, after describing Meredith, that it must be a terrible humiliation for a man who gloried in physical excellence to suffer from such a disease as *Locomotor ataxy*, that terrible jerking stammer of the hands and feet. Shaw assented briefly. Soon after, happening to look out of the window and catching sight of a large building with big windows, obviously not a block of flats, I asked him what it was. His face contracted with intense and painful sympathy and he said: 'It is a place where they torture animals. I can hardly bear the sight of it'. Now the serenity of his sympathy with the sufferings of an old man of genius and this poignant response to the pain inflicted on animals with a view to discovering remedies for human beings seemed to me to reveal a strange sense of proportion that I was often to encounter in one form or another in Shaw's works.

As I walked away I said to myself 'What is it that has made my first meeting with this man of genius different from my first meetings with others?' and I must have covered a good deal of ground before the answer flashed upon me. He had not flattered me. All the others, by graciously receiving my homage, had in a certain measure done that. Moreover I also felt that in the case of Shaw I should be recalled only when to do so was relevant to some matter which was preoccupying him; that I should be kept in a pigeon-hole and that his thoughts would never stray, as it were, accidentally in my direction.

I was destined to see him at intervals, some of them few and far between, up to 1940. My connection with *The New Statesman* as its dramatic critic and later as its literary editor (1920-1927) occasionally brought me in contact with him. I have little doubt that it was on his recommendation that I was first taken on. At a week-end party given by the Webbs at a hotel near Beachy Head to the future staff of *The New Statesman*, Shaw was also present. He arrived late in the evening and explained that he had been delayed by his mother's funeral. One of his first remarks as he settled down on the sofa before the fire was to the effect that the military understood well the kind of music that was wanted at a funeral; on the way to the grave a solemn dead march and on the way back from it a gay and rousing tune. Then with that sensitiveness that was marked in him to the impression that he might be making on others, he added after a pause: 'But don't think that I am a man who forgets the dead'. This I am sure was perfectly true, but there was something in him that made him take death more lightly than all but the very heartless—his own included, I expect.

But what I loved in Shaw was his instinctive chivalry, which, I have no doubt, exaggerated beyond all bounds his horror at using a helpless guinea-pig, dog or rabbit to discover remedies for human suffering. I was to run up against indications of this chivalry as frequently as his generosity in helping people with money. (By the way I never appealed to him on behalf of others in vain and once his contribution was so large that, to his amazement, I sent half of it back. He told me that I was a fool and that I would soon be writing to him again, but our unfortunate friend died too soon for that so I did save some of his money.) Let me record two instances of what I mean by his chivalry. I remember reading a letter by Shaw to *The Times*—I have forgotten what he was writing about, but it was not many months after the Crippen trial. In the course of this letter he casually observed 'as in the case of Mr Crippen who you may remember was a miserable hen-pecked little doctor who has been hanged for poisoning his wife'. *Mr* Crippen! The papers had been full of gloating comments on Crippen, Crippen, Crippen, as a monster beyond the pale of human sympathy and Shaw still treated him with the courtesy proper to a fellow human being. And this from the man who at the same time was constantly shocking people with his apparent off-hand insensibility, as for example with his comments on the disaster of the 'Titanic' and indeed on many other public calamities. And here is a tiny but perhaps significant instance of a sense of proportion that may be described as chivalrous and was certainly sound. It concerned myself. Shaw had persuaded me to employ a small tailor in Ireland. "You have only got to buy a roll of cloth and send him an old coat and he'll turn out just as good a suit as you'll get by going to a West End tailor and being marked all over with little bits of chalk'. I took his advice and the results were quite satisfactory, by my standards at any rate. About a month later I got a postcard from Shaw saying that as I had not paid the tailor he had done so. He knew that a young man of my habits delayed such payments. He added that I would probably be offended by his officiousness and implied that that was neither here nor there. I respected him all the more but I kept him waiting so long that when one day I met him in the street and gave him £4 10s. he had forgotten all about it. These are trifling incidents but they are symptomatic of something in Bernard Shaw which I deeply admired and made his indifference to ruthlessness on the part of dictators all the more strange.

The absence in him of personal touchiness was remarkable. I knew that I should never lose his goodwill whatever I wrote about his plays though he might think me a fool for my pains. In this respect he was a great contrast to Barrie, with whom I was also on friendly terms. In criticising one of Barrie's plays I liked if possible to read what I proposed to say to some one who knew him better in case there was a phrase or two that would deeply wound him. I remember striking out a sentence in which I had defined him as part boy, part woman, and part leprechaun with no man in him at all. Shaw would have been perfectly indifferent to any attempt to sum him up.

When *The New Statesman*, which he helped to finance, was started what he looked forward to most was the opportunity it would give him for commenting on current events anonymously in leaders. It must be remembered that at that date many were in the habit of discounting what he wrote under his own name. His general reputation then always reminded me of those lines that Bunyan wrote about himself:

> But some there be that say he laughs too loud
> And some do say his head is in a cloud.
> Some say his words and stories are so dark
> They know not by them to find his mark.

Clifford Sharp, the young editor, endeavoured to persuade him to sign his articles which was precisely what Shaw did not want to do and when he refused, rather than present them anonymously as the opinions of the paper, this young man in his twenties used to slash and cut them unmercifully. For a time Shaw bore it all with extraordinary patience and it was without resentment that he finally gave up. I know of no other literary man of anything like his eminence who would have taken such treatment so good-naturedly.

What puzzled some people about Shaw was that although in print and conversation he had far fewer inhibitions than most men about conveying intimate information to do with himself and his life, he also gave the impression that he was not more intimate with old friends than with acquaintances or indeed, one may say, with the public. I remember going to see Conrad soon after Shaw had visited him for the first time. Conrad had been shocked and almost insulted by what he considered on Shaw's part an abuse of intimacy, 'What do you think he told me? He told me that his father drank like a fish! Imagine my feelings on being presented with this revelation of his private life on our first meeting!' Conrad no doubt was a romantically fastidious Pole who instinctively took account of the milestones on the road to intimacy and it was precisely the milestones that Shaw ignored. That by the way is also a characteristic of the saint who may make no distinction in communication between those to whom they are deeply attached and human beings in general. But for all that it is disconcerting to human beings to feel that they must always be equidistant from one whom they admire. It is a trait which suggests a complete spiritual independence even perhaps of affection.

Next to his wife his closest friendship was probably with the Webbs.